PREFACE

I've been a nurse for 35 years and as the daughter of two ageing parents. I've seen that taking proactive measures to forestall future problems can make life easier. And ignoring increasing reality makes for difficulties. The unforeseen, the sudden events that fall from the heavens cannot be anticipated but a lot of the 'problems' that came with getting older can be avoided or lessened if a little forethought and planning is applied. Saying "it'll be alright" is not useful, struggling on in increasing difficulty results only in more difficulty and can mean more problems for your nearest and dearest to tackle. If you don't plan then decisions may need to be made in times of crisis rather than in times of calm contemplation and a rational approach with you at the helm. Other people may need to get involved in making your decisions for you...and they may not even be the people you like or trust or even know.

So...think about this now, plan for the future, give your relatives an easier time and most importantly, future proof yourself as much as you are able so that your life as an elder is as good as possible, doing what you prefer, how you prefer it and having as good a time as possible to boot.

INTRODUCTION

Stoicism, that ancient virtue, so easily tips into stupidity when people refuse to face facts. And getting older is a fact. It is happening to each and every one of us on this planet whilst we're alive. For some of us, getting older will also bring health problems, some of those can be prevented or alleviated if dealt with in good time. It is this that is the sticking point for some folk who are getting older and frailer but refuse to make life easy for themselves and others. The Stoic life is all very well but it doesn't increase your virtue points if you're suffering. Aging is going to happen to you... don't hide your head in the sand and think that it is just for 'other people'. The likelihood is that you are not going to wake up dead one day in your very advanced years, rather a slow decline. And though that scenario fills none of us with joy, but it doesn't have to be like that. You can change how that looks and plays out.

Life expectancy in the UK, if you reach age 65 is a further 18 and a half years for men and twenty one years for women. If you've just hit the magic number of 65, the thought of twenty-one years of baking cakes and putting the hoover round or eighteen years of sitting in the allotment shed or down the canal fishing may not fill you with glee. All that time! Don't you think we ought to do something with it? Something useful for us and hopefully useful for society as a whole? Something that is fun? Something that we've always wanted to do? Something that challenges us a bit and expands our lives and our mental horizons? By all means sit around watching soap operas or raising turnips for the rest of your life if that's what fills you with glee, but really...all that time is a fabulous opportunity to get cracking on something really marvellous...the latter part of your life!

Being a hospital based nurse, the folk of elder years I usually see, are il but that doesn't reflect the truth of older people. Occasionally, if I'm working on a surgical ward, I meet someone who is 95 and it's their first time in a hospital and they're only in because they need a hernia repair. Take the case of my great uncle who at 94 was refused a hip replacement on the NHS because the surgeon thought it was a waste and someone younger would get more use out of it. Uncle Alf had it done privately, made an excellent recovery and lived healthily, walking daily and attending dances till he was 98. There are people out there, living proof that life as an older person does not need to be a packet of misery. They are some of them lucky...they don't have any serious health concerns. Not all of them though. I have also met patients who come into hospital regularly for various conditions but who also maintain a positive 'can do' attitude. Don't let your age or other people's expectations of you dictate what you do on a daily basis. If you've had a yen to do Delhi to Tashkent overland for years, now is the time to give that a really serious examination and make it happen. If you want to write the book, start now. If you want to do a degree in philosophy, Anglo-Saxon literature or advanced physics, now is the time. There are a million and one things we could do. Seize the day.

This book is relevant for those in the UK, the legalities differ in other countries and therefore I can't give specific advice for such.

I've divided this book into chapters, dip in and out, pick and mix as you will or read it from front to back. I hope it will give you pause for thought and enable you to take control of your life and your elder years. I've used references in this book that are available in the ordinary world of the internet and easy to access academic tomes. I want something to be available for you to check and see what else is written on the subject. There are a few academic papers that I have used for references but again, these are easily available and don't need payment or membership of an academic establishment either. I've checked the links recently and aim to do it at least annually in the future so that they stay relevant. At the end of chapters I have collated the references or the websites that I have used and listed them with a brief explanation of each one as a signpost should you wish to further investigate yourself. My hope is that if you read this and you can avoid some of the common pitfalls, some of the unfortunate events that can occur, then you can live into your elder years having fun and a great time.

We will achieve more if we plan for a happy and healthy 'old age'. By taking a proactive stance. By embracing life while we still have it. By living our best regardless of wrinkles, a less than perfect abdomen and varicose veins, achy hips and a need for hearing aids. By shining as an example of what is possible. By showing what can be done and having fun whilst we're at it.

CHAPTER 1

Future Proofing

I'm going to start this book with a short chapter on looking at where you are now in an effort to forestall what might happen in the future. Bear in mind here that none of us knows what the future will bring, (possible exceptions being Christmas and taxes) but having been around on this earth for some time, you will have got the gist of how life usually pans out. It involves getting older. Statistically there are a lot of us Oldsters about now, in the UK we make up approximately 20% of the population [1] and that percentage is going to increase. The rate is roughly the same for the USA [2], Australia is slightly lower at 15% [3], New Zealand at 13% [4]. You get the idea, there's a fair few of us around. And traditionally 'old age' (which is in itself a term that means very little, lets stick to statistical stuff here and say that I'm writing this book for folks who are 60 and over) brings with it some problems and ill health. As we are tending to live longer as a population, we are more likely to encounter some form of ill health during that time. Ideally we wouldn't and there are folk who live a hale and hearty 'old age' and shuffle off this mortal coil with no more than a day or two of illness, but most of us will encounter a bit of ill health. So, this chapter is about forward planning and thinking about what might happen. Not what is going to happen, none of us knows that...but statistically you are likely to run into some sort of health trouble as you get older. Start thinking about how you want your life to be and to plan for eventualities.

I suggest a good place to start is with 'where you are now' from the point of view of diet, housing, health, finances, possessions, social engagement. Have a deep think about those particular headings, I'm not suggesting you drive yourself into a fit of despair but if you're still smoking/ vaping/ indulging in recreational drugs/ drinking excess alcohol/ binge eating then this could be the ideal opportunity to take charge of your health and to sally forth into your older years in the best shape you've been. The same goes for where you are living, how much stuff you've got and whether it's being a bit of a trial rather than useful, finances...anyway, let's deal with it bit by bit.

Diet

There is a fair amount of research readily available in the public domain to prove that the usual diet we eat is not actually that good for us and leads to inflammation. I'm not going to advocate

---

[1] https://www.ons.gov.uk/peoplepopulationandcommunity/populationandmigration/populationestimates/articles/overviewoftheukpopulation/2020 Accessed 3rd January 2022, checked 26th December 2023

[2] https://www.suddenlysenior.com/senior-facts-and-figures/ Accessed 3rd January 2022, checked 26th December 2023

[3] https://www.aihw.gov.au/reports-data/population-groups/older-people/overview Accessed 3rd January 2022, checked 26th December r2023

[4] https://countrymeters.info/en/New_Zealand Accessed 3rd January 2022, checked 26th December 2023

one particular method of eating or dietary plan over another, it behoves you to investigate. Find out what the latest research is around food and dietary intake. Don't necessarily believe everything that the mainstream promotes – remember that a 'low fat' diet was touted for over two decades as the proper way to eat [5] [6], turns out it doesn't actually do us any good and may well be responsible for a lot of unintended and malign consequences. You know your body well enough by now to know what causes direct results, what gives you wind, what keeps you awake at night, what makes your knees ache. What you may not be aware of is the link between dietary intake and a lot of other symptoms that you may not readily think of as being dietary related. Such symptoms as skin rashes and pain, depression and poor sleep. Amongst the many culprits could be chilli sauce, coffee, red meat and nightshade vegetables (tomatoes, potatoes, aubergine, peppers, sweet potatoes) [7] alcohol and simple sugars [8] [9]. Do some homework and some research around this and find out if there is anything you can do from the point of view of food intake that will make your physical life any better. It is never too late to amend a way of eating and taking up a healthier one. Though you think you may not benefit and 'what's the point?', you may surprise yourself by feeling better in as little as a week by eating well. If you have a chronic disease that is diet related (coeliac disease, diabetes) reassess your diet and think if you could up your game a bit and eat even better.

Housing

Where do you live? Are you happy there? Have you always wanted to move? Well now seems like as good time a time as any. Is your domicile becoming too much for you to realistically manage? Move into a smaller house. If you have the beginnings of mobility problems then think about moving now, before you have to move or you get limited to living in one room. So many people leave this till it is too late to move and gain any benefit, always better to take action and move and enjoy your new abode and get settled in. Don't hide your head in the sand on this one, I've seen lots of people come a cropper with this because they didn't want to face the reality. If realistically, you are facing a deterioration of health then get the domestic situation sorted out sooner and don't leave this one in the hope that one day you will wake up with all your facilities restored.

Could the house/ bungalow/ flat be modified to make it easier to live in as you age and possibly become more infirm? Get the bathroom updated, get the kitchen made good to live in with a

---

[5] https://www.mayoclinichealthsystem.org/hometown-health/speaking-of-health/10-nutrition-myths-debunked 13th December 2021, checked 26th December 2023

[6] Weinberg, Sylvan Lee, 'The Diet-Heart Hypothesis' Journal of the American College of Cardiology, Vol 43, no.5, 2004 730-733 accessed via https://www.sciencedirect.com/science/article/pii/S0735109703016310 on 13th December 2021, checked 26th December 2023

[7] Juhasz, Francine, 'Are There Certain Foods That Cause Muscle nd Joint Pain?' accessed via https://www.livestrong.com/article/330792-food-that-causes-muscle-joint-pain/ 13th December 2021, checked 26th December 2023

[8] https://www.hopkinsmedicine.org/health/conditions-and-diseases/psoriasis-diet-foods-to-eat-and-avoid-if-you-have-psoriasis Accessed 26th December 2023

[9] https://www.livestrong.com/article/13772283-foods-bad-for-skin/ Accessed 26th December 2023

wheelchair if that's what you need, get electrical sockets put in, get the lighting upgraded so you're not stumbling around in the dark and gloom all the time. Get those rugs up off the floor…they're a trip hazard and falls kill people (not necessarily instantly). If you live in rented accommodation, now is the time to alert your landlord if repairs and 'making good' needs to be done. If it is starting to be a little difficult to do stuff think if there's anything that could be done to make it easier. If the shower needs improving, get on to them now. If the taps leak, deal with it immediately. Likewise any structural faults in the building (regardless of whether you rent or own). Your house is merely the physical extension of where you live, get it sorted as soon as possible.

Health

Get your routine tests done regularly, don't leave them and think that you'll do them later or postpone or ignore them because they are problematic to attend. Do them when the appointment arrives or the stool testing kit drops through the letter box. Avidly chase up the results so that you are aware of what's going on with your body. I deal with opticians and audiology in detail later on in this book, but yes, keep up with their appointments. Keep up to date with immunisations too and I'm not just meaning Covid 19. Also get your annual 'flu jab if you can….'flu is a nasty disease and does kill people (even young and fit people). If you need regular B12 injections then ensure you're on somebody's list to get them done. If you have diabetes, go for your check ups every time and see the ophthalmologists and chiropodist annually. Diabetes is not a disease to be taken lightly.

Being proactive with your health firstly consists of facing up to what is happening in all its messiness and general grot. Look, we all feel physically fabulous at the age of 25, it takes no intelligence and very little in the way of imagination. You want to go climb a mountain, no problems, go do it. You want to ride your bike all the way to the coast and back in a day…fine. Nature has set us up to feel fine and fantastic, generally look buff so we can attract a mate and reproduce, have the stamina to cope with parenting and / or putting food on the table and keeping the whole shebang going. When it begins to get difficult is as we age. Research is showing with increasing regularity that we start aging a lot sooner than we originally realised [10]. I mean on one side, yes of course we're aging from the moment we are born but what I'm talking about here are the physical effects of the process. The loss of muscle power, stamina, various faculties become a dim and distant memory, things start 'going south'. Paradoxically we tend to treat this in a twofold manner. When dealing with professionals or folk that are in a position to help us, we blithely say "old age doesn't come alone" so that we give the impression of stoically embracing the challenges. Left to ourselves and in private we tend not to think about what is to come, how much we've changed and how that is going to pan out. There is a certain amount of ignoring what might be coming. Just putting up with things and conditions because that's how they are is all very well, but

---

[10] Besdine, Richard W, 'Changes in the Body with Aging' accessed via https://www.southportland.org/files/8615/0470/1756/Changes_in_the_Body_with_Aging.pdf
26th December 2023

it's not exactly taking charge of your life is it? It's not preparing for how things could be and it's certainly not trying to forestall any problems afore they arise.

So, I am advocating that you start thinking about this subject, wherever you are on the getting older continuum. Be you twenty and zinging around like a kitten on speed, fifty and feeling a little weary at the end of the day or eighty-five and absolutely shattered. Because every single one of us no matter how old we are has the ability to feel a little better about the subject (note that I don't say that we have the ability to feel better *per se*, I don't want to lead you up the garden path here with promises that all will be alright, your pain will go away, you'll be able to do cartwheels again and you'll wake up 25 again in a few weeks). And surely, that is a condition to be embraced. Feeling better about the whole thing, having a little more hope and positivity about things.

If you have the time to sit and watch television then you have the time to devote to actively researching this subject so as to give yourself the best knowledge possible. If you have the internet at home then you can do it. I advocate learning all you can about the aging process so you are in a position of power and knowledge and can figure out what is best for you.

Social inclusion

One thing I have heard older folks say is that there are less people to talk to. If they've lost a partner, the children have long since grown up and gone, the grandchildren are out in the world making their way...who is there to talk to? And whilst we're on this subject can I just intervene here to comment on the bizarre belief that sometimes occurs when suggestions such as 'lunch clubs' and day centres are suggested as ways of increasing social contact, to whit "But they're for old people"....er, yes, and you are one. Think of the benefits of meeting up with a group of folk from the same generation...they know exactly what you're talking about when you mention Diana Rigg's leather body suit in 'The Avengers', they understand completely why you adore (or despise) the music of Abba, they can talk and converse about cultural icons in common. If you continually ignore people of your own age, you are just reinforcing the belief that old people are not interesting and have nothing to say (nothing to say? Ha....I can't even write my autobiography because it's too incriminating....don't give me "old people aren't interesting"). If you are unable to make conversation with someone you've just been introduced to because they're 'too old', I think that says a lot about your conversational ability and self-belief. Shape up, you're a member of the human tribe. Are you implying with your belief that 'it's for old people', that elders have nothing interesting to say? Are you implying that your life and experience count for nothing? Or are you saying that you are conversationally backward and can't be bothered to make conversation with other people? Why then, should people be bothered making conversation with you? Right, have you felt my passion on this one? One cannot complain of lack of conversationalists unless you live totally in splendid isolation with absolutely no family, neighbours, friends and you literally see no one from day to day. Now I know that for some people this is how it is...so if you yearn for social inclusion and or a bit of a chat, get yourself off to a lunch club or get your social worker to refer you to one. Ask local charities for a befriending service visit. I've included a list of resources at the end of this chapter.

Can I mention here that the telephone works both ways. Don't sit at home wondering why the children and/ or grandchildren never ring you and sulking and feeling aggrieved about it…get on the blower and ring them. If the timing is out and they're busy with other things, the phone will go to ansaphone and you can leave a message, it may be they are actually glad to hear from you and charmed by your desire to know how their life is getting on.

Those of you that live alone and in conditions of 'social isolation' and don't see folk from one day to the next…now it's possible that some of you like it that way and if that's the case, please carry on. Ensure you keep in contact with important folk, your next of kin, significant people in your life, the doctor, the dentist, anyone who provides a service that you use but totally withdrawing from the heady round of life, though providing calm and space for thought, mustn't be allowed to slide into loneliness, agoraphobia or general sociopathy. In other words…make a bit of an effort here, even if it's just to let folk know you're still alive and kicking.

Those of you who may find loneliness the major bane of life (and it can be such) will need to make an effort to go out and get involved in things. You cannot sit at home and expect the world to come beating a path to your door. And getting involved in things means either going out of the house and joining in with social groups or initiating contact by phone or e mail. Yes, you will have to push yourself a bit here and get out of your comfort zone…but isn't that what life is all about? If you stay still, you're going backwards. You may just meet a new best friend, a new life partner, a new lover, a new surrogate daughter or son. Just do it. If you go to a meeting of a group and don't like it, you have at least been outdoors. And met some new people. And you don't have to go back there if it wasn't to your taste. Just keep trying.

Social isolation is not to be taken lightly and I am not intending to do so here. There are a lot of charities that provide excellent help in this area, from the befriending service I mentioned above to various clubs and day centres. I give some references at the end of this chapter to investigate if you want to do so. Don't let any physical constraints prevent you, most things can be dealt with by planning. If transport is a problem, then the organising facilities of various clubs or charities may be able to provide such. It is worth investigating because as a society we are so much more aware since the advent of Covid, of how very important it is to be connected with one's tribe. We are a social animal; we need to be in contact with each other.

Finances

For all of the purported power of the 'grey pound' [11] in which apparently a lot of us over 50's wield a fair bit of financial clout, the reality is that for a lot of us, poverty is real [12] [13]. Certainly, with recent events on the world stage (Covid, the hike in fuel costs, the increase in food costs), money goes less far. There are large number of us that live in poverty. If this is you, take the advice of AgeUK and check to see if you are eligible for any financial help from the state. Is there any way you can safely lessen your outgoings? Note the optimum word here is safely. The idea is to remain fed, sheltered and warm, the latter is important as a cold house can lead to ill health in an elder whereas in a younger person it would not necessarily do so [14].

There are a few things that can lead to elder poverty, not planning for an adequate pension is one of them and hopefully this will lessen as the years roll on and folk are enrolled into employer's pension schemes. For many of us when we were younger, a pension was for people who were paid enough to contribute to one and most of us poorer paid population must rely on the state pension. Unfortunately there are also scammers who prey on older folk who may not have quite so much interweb savvy. And of course, there are family who may persistently ask to borrow money or even steal it. I don't mean to paint a bleak picture here but this is the reality that some folk have to deal with. If you are in the position of being in debt or unable to afford the essentials and basics of life, reach out to the various helping agencies. I've mentioned AgeUK who are a very good resource when dealing with this, they have a calculator to help work out what benefits may be payable, have information about keeping well and an advice line. It is also worth while telephoning your fuel provider if your costs are too great. They really are not interested in keeping people in the cold and dark, they would far rather hear from you and try to help you figure out the problems. Some county councils also run a helpline for dealing with fuel costs and can help with trying to get a better deal.

Possessions

Possessions, love them or hate them, we all need a certain amount of them. And as you get older, you may not need so many, certainly if you curtail social activities or the number of hobbies you have. There is a very cathartic joy to clearing the clutter, giving yourself a bit more space in the home and just generally allowing a breeze to blow through (a metaphorical one, I'm not suggesting you do away with curtains, doors or window glazing). Spend some time thinking about what you

---

[11] https://rejuvage.com/power-grey-pound/ Accessed 5th January 2022, checked 26th December 2023

[12] https://www.theguardian.com/society/2019/aug/18/elderly-poverty-risen-fivefold-since-80s-pensions Accessed 5th January 2022, checked 26th December 2023 but note this article is over 4 years old (still, I don't reckon much has changed)

[13] https://www.ageuk.org.uk/latest-press/articles/2021/number-of-pensioners-living-in-poverty-tops-two-million/ Accessed 5th January 2022, checked 26t December 2023

[14] https://www.beatcold.org.uk/how-fuel-poverty-affects-the-elderly/ Accessed 10th January 2022, c checked 26th December 2023

actually need and what is just there because it's just there. So, for instance, if you're saving your best Wedgewood china bowls to leave to your granddaughter and you no longer use them, give them to her now. If you're saving all the family documents to be handed on to your eldest son, do it now. Jewellery left in a jewellery box on a dressing table and never worn is a waste. Give it to your eldest daughter if she expresses a liking for it. You may well get to see and delight in her wearing it. Going through all the many, many pairs of shoes you have that you can no longer wear will lead to a trip down Memory Lane but ultimately you can give them away to people who need them (or you can sell them on EBay and make some money) and save your relatives from the necessity of sorting through heaps of shoes that mean nothing to them. And clear out your closet so that you can see what you do actually have. This process can take as long or as short a time as you like but it will prove beneficial. You will benefit from going through all these things you have collected and revisiting the memories, and those left behind eventually will benefit as they will not need to trawl through room upon room of mouldering, moth eaten stuff that means nothing to them (been there, done that). You know there is a reason that minimalism is such a popular trope and that is because it enables a life with more freedom and sense of space.

I am not suggesting that you need to crack on with this immediately. If the whole idea of doing it fills you with dread then think about what would make it easier for you. Inviting a favourite grandchild to help? Asking your daughter to devote an hour a week to helping you? Doing your home one drawer at a time? There is no set agenda or timetable for this but it is a procedure that really would benefit you and make life so much easier for those left behind who will be dealing with grief and arrangements and not in a good 'place' for deciding what happens to your prized collection of Dinky toys.

Logistics

Sometimes with age comes a lessening of ability to do things, everyday tasks that were previously so routine as to not even be thought of or commented upon. And because age related infirmity creeps up slowly, we tend to make do and manage when really we may be better served by analysing what we're doing and what we're trying to achieve. Various tasks spring to mind: taking plugs out of sockets that are just above the skirting board, reaching into the back of a wall mounted cupboard in the kitchen, getting the ironing board out of the airing cupboard, hanging the washing up, lifting heavy pots and pans, opening jars. You may have your own little bugbears that you don't even notice apart from they irritate you a little as they take more time. So, I recommend having a bit of a think about what is proving to be a nuisance, what is taking more time, is being more of a difficulty and figuring out ways around the problem.

For a start, storage places of everyday, commonly used items could be changed so that there is easier access and you don't have to try to get to the back of a cupboard. Tea bags or the coffee pot could live on the work surface nearer the kettle rather than stashed away in a cupboard. I understand the aesthetic allure of a bare work surface but function comes first, it has to work for you and to make your life easier. Electrical sockets can be raised further up the wall, or more can be put in at a higher level to make life easier. If your house hasn't been updated recently and you find you are having to use extension leads or plugs, that is a good sign that you need more sockets, not leads trailing across the floor which are indeed a trip hazard.

Could the ironing board live elsewhere? Could you get someone else to do the ironing if it is too much for you? Or could you (only a suggestion) confine ironing to the very bare essentials (outer apparel only) and leave the big stuff such a sheets or duvet covers unironed? A shirt is only seen at the front if a jacket is worn, likewise a blouse if a cardigan is over top it. Therefore only those bits need to be ironed really. I am not suggesting that you do this unless it is a problem for you to do the ironing, there are some of us that love the occasion to bring order to laundry chaos and if you are one and you can still do it, please, continue onwards.

Heavy pots and pans? Could they live out on the work surface near the stove? If lifting them when they are full is a problem then consider getting lighter weight ones and passing on your heavy cookware to someone else. The same goes for your heavy china or glass dishes, they are not much use sitting in a cupboard if they're too heavy to use. Pass them on to someone else and get something lighter and more manageable.

I have noticed some some folks are reluctant to engage with change. Any change. From changing the place where the tea bags are stored to changing the day of shopping delivery to changing abode when it is apparent that climbing up three flights of stairs with a wheelchair is not going to happen. It is this reluctance to change and to embrace what is one of the very characteristics of life that leads to ossification of viewpoint, ability and eventually mental agility. All life is change, every moment is change. There is nothing to be gained from trying to hang on to what is or what has been when it no longer serves you. It is akin to hanging on to clothes from 30 years and 3 stones ago because you don't want to change. Certainly, as one gets older and possibly needs help in the form of carers or even one's relatives, change will need to occur to allow other people's commitments to be met. Carers will not always arrive at the same time due to traffic problems or an ill client. Your child may not be able to run at your beck and call because they are looking after their children or going to the dentist or any one of the myriad little things that life is made from.

I can understand that a routine is a comfort but when it becomes a tyrannical timetable that you and everyone else has to meet, then it is no longer a help but a problem. A way to forestall the possible unnerving sensation that a change of routine may induce is to bring about the change yourself. Spend time evaluating your surroundings and environment and think if there are ways you can make life easier or more streamlined for yourself and/ or your carers or those who are coming in to help. Certain things may become more troublesome or difficult as time goes by, rather than struggle on, think about how you could improve that situation and how it could be made easier. Use a bit of imagination regarding where things of everyday utility are kept. There is no hard and fast rule for this, you know your domestic set up, you know what you want to achieve throughout the day. Could it be made any easier by changing where things are kept? By changing your routine? By changing your grocery delivery supplier? A prime example is insurance. Car and house insurance providers routinely increase their premiums year on year and you as the loyal customer think no more of this practice than it is probably to meet rising costs. Well, start investigating how much it would cost with other suppliers because you may well save yourself hundreds of pounds. Your reluctance to deal with change is what the insurance providers are banking on, that you won't investigate how much cheaper it is elsewhere. Don't forget that you as the consumer can vote with your purse – but that may require embracing a bit of change.

The reluctance to change leads to what I refer to as ossification, taking on a rigid and bone like structure. Bones do not malleably bend with changing circumstances, too much pressure and they break. Avoid this scenario by adopting the practice of regularly evaluating your routines, your life, your home environment, all of it to see if you can make things easier.

Conclusion

I've briefly skirted various topics that I think bear analysis as one gets older and possibly more infirm (it's not a given though) and I hope they've helped. Or at least given you food for thought and an idea of what might benefit from a bit of arranging or sorting out. I'll close this chapter with a list of resources, folk you can access online or phone to get help or advice if you need it

Useful websites and resources

https://wwwactionforelders.org.uk is a Cardiff based charity that focuses on "adding life to later life", they provide free online exercise activities and some classes held in the community. There is also a video library of exercise classes. They have an online book club (via Zoom) which holds monthly meetings and they provide online guides to using the internet and staying connected safely with a member of their team dedicated to getting folks up and running on the interweb if it's new to them.

https://www.ageuk.org.uk/ is the UK's leading charity dealing with aging, they provide a myriad of useful things, a helpline (0800 678 1602, available every day from 8am until 7pm), huge amounts of information on a massive amount of subjects that are roughly grouped together as 'Money & legal; Health & wellbeing; Care & support; Work & learning', they run a telephone befriending service and a 'real life' befriending service, can put you in touch with your local group who may well know of a local handyperson, they run day centres, provide personal alarm services and stairlift information and sell incontinence products.

https://www.charitychoice.co.uk have a list of charities by sector. They do a lot around the elder group but you can also search by postcode so you can find local ones or browse by charity sector for such areas as Armed and Ex Services or Disabled or Mental Health.

https://cinnamon.org.uk/ is a charity that concerns itself with the care of pets of elder people (or terminally ill people) who find themselves through illness or infirmity, unable to cope or care for their domestic animals. They can provide dog walkers and are adept at rehoming pets due to illness, death or admission to non-pet friendly places.

https://www.jrf.org.uk/ The JRF (Joseph Rowntree Foundation) and the Joseph Rowntree Housing Trust is 'an independent social change organisation working to solve UK poverty'. It doesn't deal with just elders but it publishes articles on a regular basis dealing with poverty in all its forms in the UK. It actively engages to promote ways to decrease poverty for all people in the UK and its articles make useful reading around the subject.

https://www.reengage.org.uk is a charity (previously known as Contact the Elderly) devoted to providing 'social connections for older people at a time in their lives when their social circles are diminishing'. They run tea parties (with transport there and back), a telephone befriending service, activity groups (some face to face, others on line). They have a freephone number on 0800 716543

https://www.salvatoionarmy.org.uk the well-known Christian charity that put their emphasis on action, they will help with later life by providing various clubs (including walking clubs, lunch clubs, meet up clubs, community choirs, sports, gardening clubs), opportunities to volunteer, various courses to increase knowledge around elder years and Christian teaching programmes. They also have twelve residential care homes and one day centre in the UK and Ireland.

https://www.silverline.org.uk are open 24 hours a day and provide a telephone service matching volunteers to older people, they can refer callers on to other sources of support and importantly they can provide support to elders suffering abuse or neglect. Their number is 0800 470 8090.

CHAPTER 2

Aids and adjuncts that may help

As one ages, things may deteriorate…. hearing, sight, to a certain extent smell and taste in some folk. So in this chapter I'm going to deal with the senses and talk about services available and taking care of various accoutrements, aids and bits and bobs that can help.

Eyes

We think nothing of getting a pair of glasses to help us keep doing the activities we love…sewing, soldering, writing birthday cards to grandchildren, cracking safes and sudoku and dare I say it for sounding hideously antiquated…reading a good book. I'm sure that most people own more than one pair and (whisper it quietly lest we be thought frivolous) match them to our colour scheme and mood and occasion. A work pair, an at home pair, a driving pair, a 'being in the handbag pair,' the use of specs is ubiquitous and praise be that we live in an age where we have such good facilities and knowledge of eyes. Really…most of us would say with the least prompting "I'm lost without my glasses" or more commonly "I used to have perfect eyesight".

Have your eyes tested regularly, if you're over 60 it is free so aim for every two years. If you have glaucoma or diabetes, get them checked annually [15]. Don't omit or postpone because this is important stuff, you keeping yourself as well, active and in the loop as possible is what we're aiming for here. With delays, you could be losing sight. Without eyesight you have less agency in life, it means not driving, not seeing your computer, television or phone screen, not seeing pictures of your grandchildren, your favourite rose in the garden or the latest racy series on telly and never quite getting around to reading 'War and Peace'. So get it done.

If you can't get to the optometrist due to disability then they can come to you [16]. The NHS website is a good resource to find what you may be entitled to and there can be help with meeting the cost of lenses [17], your optician may be able to advise.

Take care of your glasses too, you'll have paid some money for them, so ensure that you don't put them lens down on a surface for fear of scratching those lenses. If the little screws in the frames fall out or come loose, take them (or post them if mobility or your location makes visiting difficult) to the optician with whom you deal and get them mended. Usually a little repair can be done on the spot but even if you have to leave them for a day or so, it is worth it to have a pair of serviceable glasses. Clean your glasses with a proper lens cleaning cloth, one will have been

---

[15] https://www.nhs.uk/nhs-services/opticians/free-nhs-eye-tests-and-optical-vouchers Accessed 7th December 2023

[16] https://www.nhs.uk/nhs-services/opticians/free-nhs-eye-tests-and-optical-vouchers Accessed 7th December 2023

[17] https://www.nhs.uk/nhs-services/opticians/free-eye-tests-and-optical-vouchers Accessed 7th December 2023

provided in the glasses case when you were given your latest new pair. Do this daily (at least) and it's worth doing it a few times a day as they get grubbier and grubbier as the day goes on, though subtly so you don't notice. Research has shown that bacteria grow on spectacle frames and lenses so clean them [18], impregnated lens wipes were most effective but even a dry cloth helps. It is the frames that are most at risk of bacteria, the lenses less so [19], you could try using tepid tap water and a dry scratch free cloth to clean them. When not in use, keep your spectacles in their case for protection.

If you are prescribed a particular course of eye drops or eye cream for various conditions, you are really only fooling yourself if you don't do as the instructions request. Eye care needs to be taken seriously so whilst it may be an inconvenience to put drops into your eyes four times a day, just do it! Be aware that some eye drops will need to be kept in the fridge once opened and best practice if you need them in both eyes is to have a separate bottle for each eye (label them so you don't get them mixed up) so that you don't transfer any potential infection from one eye to another. If putting eye drops in is a difficult procedure for you there are ways to make it easier. Lie down for a start, saves the strain on your neck and gives the drop time to make its way around your eyeball. There are a few nifty gadgets to help you administer drops [20] if you find it difficult. Also advised is to stay laying down for two minutes after you've put the eye drops in so that they do have time to really do the job for which they are intended.

Hearing

So, on to hearing aids. If your family, colleagues, friends, people you meet in the course of the day tell you you're going deaf or you need your hearing tested, they are probably not gaslighting you. They think you really are and you really do. Let me illustrate. My husband told me a few times during heated domestic conversations (you know what I mean!!) during my 40's that I needed my hearing tested. I didn't believe him but I'm such a contrarian that I went to the doctors and asked for an audiology appointment (that's how you go about getting it, go to the GP and ask and tell them why- they are unlikely to accept your word, they'll want to know what prompted you to ask for a hearing test). I duly showed up to that appointment (I live in a devolved country that takes the health of its' population seriously so I got that appointment pretty swiftly). Turns out I needed bilateral (both sides) hearing aids as I had a mild to moderate hearing deficit. Ah, how galling, it turns out my husband was right! A few months later, I was fitted with my first of the two and went home. It being a sunny day and warm, we decided to have tea in the garden and I realised, I could

---

[18] Fritz et al., *'A View to a Kill?- Ambient bacterial load of frames and lenses of spectacles and evaluation of different cleaning methods'*, 2018, Public Library of Sciences, https://www.ncbi.nlm.nih.gov/pmc/articles/PMC6261565/ Accessed 24th May 2021 and 7th December 2023

[19] Fritz et al., *'A View to a Kill?- Ambient bacterial load of frames and lenses of spectacles and evaluation of different cleaning methods'*, 2018, Public Library of Sciences, https://www.ncbi.nlm.nih.gov/pmc/articles/PMC6261565/ Accessed 24th May 2021 and 7th December 2023

[20] In the UK a quick search on https://www.amazon.co.uk will turn up a number of them.

hear bird song. I also realised that I hadn't heard bird song for quite some while and that made me quite emotional (cue hankies).

The benefit of getting hearing aids when you need them and not a decade later when the neighbours are serving noise abatement notices on you because the TV is so loud, is that you maintain the neural pathways involved in hearing [21]. In everyday language this means that the nerves involved in hearing stay intact because they are still being put through their paces, you've got hearing aids, you wear them, the nerves pick up the sound and process it as they always did (I never fail to be amazed at the beauty of the workings of the body). Not only hearing but the fact that you are still hearing and engaged in the world means your brain is working well to maintain its functions, you have a lesser risk of developing dementia [22], less risk of falls, less incidence of depression and anxiety [23]. The ability to hear and hear well is priceless, you get to hear birdsong, music, your beloved murmuring sweet nothings to you, the cat demanding to be fed, the wind through ripe wheat when you are out for a walk, the passer-by saying good morning and the post person whistling. All these things are what go to make up a life. Communication with others is what keeps us part of this heady wheel of life, this community of souls. So when you are dealing with other people please do them the courtesy of wearing your hearing aids. I don't care if you don't like them, if you don't wear them I won't be able to speak to you in a manner that aids communication between the two of us. I don't really care that you wear them, I don't think any the less of you, in fact I think more of you. It doesn't mean that you're over the hill, it just means you have a hearing deficit and praise be, we live in an age with an understanding of audiology, hearing aids, the importance of communication. Use the facilities we have been given! (please!!).

Hearing aids can be obtained through two channels in the UK, by requesting a referral to audiology from the GP. This is the NHS service and we are all aware how very cash strapped is the whole enterprise…you may wait some time. The hearing aids they supply never actually belong to you, you are honour bound to give them back if you no longer need them and you are also honour bound to take care of them. There are a few varieties of hearing aids that can be supplied, the common behind the ear one, practically invisible ones that sit inside the ear canal, ones with tubes that go into the ear entrance and others with specially made moulds [24]. The Audiologist who does the initial hearing test with you (which takes a good twenty minutes) will advise on which sort they feel most appropriate. Some varieties are unsuitable for those with profounder hearing loss and some require a fair amount of dexterity [25]. The hearing aids will usually be supplied with a little

---

[21] https://myhearingcenters.com/blog/if-i-can-still-hear-is-it-ok-to-put-off-getting-hearing-aids/ Accessed 27th May 2021 and 7th December 2023

[22] Amieva H. et al *"Self-Reported Hearing Loss, Hearing Aids, and Cognitive Decline in Elderly Adults: A 25-Year Study"* 2015, Journal of the American Geriatrics Society accessed via https://agsjournals.onlinelibrary.wiley.com/doi/10.1111/jgs.13649/abstract;jsessionid=BE74008E2688506FD62F8092FDB30BEC.f03t03?deniedAccessCustomisedMessage=&userIsAuthenticated=false on 7th December 2023

[23] https://www.aarp.org/health/conditions-treatments/info-2019/hearing-aids-benefits.html Accessed 7th December 2023

[24] https://www.nhs.uk/conditions/hearing-aids-and-implants/ Accessed 7th December 2023

[25] https://www.nhs.uk/conditions/hearing-aids-and-implants/ Accessed 7th December 2023

cleaning kit (if you've lost it or were never given one just ring the audiology department and ask them to send you one), make a habit of cleaning your hearing aids and the moulds and tubes on a weekly basis. The good thing about this is that whilst those hearing aids never belong to you, they will get updated or mended with no charge. Don't be cavalier with them though, this is state of the art technology and worthy of your best care. Take them out before you wash your hair or go swimming (a lesson I learnt the hard way). Also worth mentioning is that with NHS ones you will get them updated if need be when you attend for routine hearing tests and the batteries are free.

The other way to go about this is to go privately. I will say two things on this latter route...first, they are trying to sell you something (at huge cost), just keep that in mind when you are going for your hearing test and consultation; secondly, those (expensive) hearing aids that you buy subsequent to your consultation will be your responsibility, so if you go into hospital, the staff will not be able to get them mended for you or supply you with batteries for them. There are however payment plans available to help with the cost of private hearing aids [26] [27] and the bonus of going private is that you won't have to wait long for your initial appointment. I have however looked after a fair few patients who expect that their hearing aids will be mended for them whilst they are in hospital (and that in itself begs the question of why they didn't get them mended whilst they were at home?) and that batteries will be supplied and the paraphernalia associated with the hearing aids, chargers, programmers, cleaning equipment can all be sorted out once someone is admitted to hospital. It can't. All the hospital staff can do is send an NHS hearing aid back to the nearest audiology department or provide batteries for an NHS hearing aid. Your privately obtained hearing aid is your property to be cared for by you.

Taste and smell

Lessening taste and smell (I'm not referring to an acute loss of both of them, I am talking here of a steady deterioration that occurs as one ages [28]... and not to everybody) can cause difficulties in later years because if food doesn't taste as good, it's not so enjoyable, one is less likely to eat. And that is a problem because if you start losing weight unintentionally as you get older, you are making yourself more liable to ill health. Now I'm not talking here about deliberate weight loss undertaken because one is larger than is healthy but if you start to notice that things don't taste as good then there are a few things you need to do. Firstly, is this a gradual onset? Just think back and work out how long this has been going on. If it is a sudden occurrence then it may be something that can be rectified, get to the doctors, get it sorted. As I alway say, do not prevaricate! If it has been a gradual onset then mention it to the doctor when you next see them and start figuring out a way round this problem, they may refer you on to a specialist if deemed appropriate as there are

---

[26] https://www.thcp.co.uk/hearing-aids/hear-now-pay-later Accessed 7th December 2023

[27] https://www.bootshearingcare.com/finance/ Accessed 7th December 2023

[28] Hazell T. *'Loss of Taste and Smell'* https://patient.info/ears-nose-throat-mouth/smell-and-taste-disorders Accessed 7th December 2023

some conditions causing this that can be rectified [29]. If food doesn't taste as good as it used to, you may want to consider increasing flavourings by using herbs and spices. I wouldn't recommend just putting more salt on everything, there are health implications in the use of too much salt [30]. Smaller amounts of everything but more variety may help. Trying different and new foods may also give a little fillip to the appetite and taste and appreciation. Traditional 'hot' cuisines, Indian, Mexican, Thai, West Indian may be worth exploring for new tastes as well. Try not to just load desserts with more sugar to make them taste better, we all know that the white poison is just that…a poison.

Teeth

Teeth are worth including in this section because some of us are lucky enough to keep our own as we age, others are more reliant on false teeth, plates, bridges and dentures. These aids to eating and enjoyment of food are just as deserving of care, a dirty pair of dentures is an aid to nothing but bad breath and ill health. Dentures and plates will come from your dentist with instructions on how to keep them clean, abide by these instructions and clean them. A good soaking in a proprietary denture cleaning is all very well but it's as good as cleaning your natural teeth by using a mouth wash and nothing else. The grime and associated bits of food that get caught in the crevices need removal by mechanical means and that's by way of a toothbrush (one can buy a special denture brush if one has the desire to but an ordinary toothbrush will suffice). Use a proprietary denture cleaner for this, artificial teeth are made of softer stuff than our natural ones and so will scratch easier if you use ordinary toothpaste with vigour [31]. Don't use washing up liquid or bleach or household cleaners.

Most of the references I have consulted recommend taking dentures out overnight, to prevent build-up of bacteria and to prevent bone loss in the lower jaw [32] but the NHS website says that's it's not always necessary but does give your gums a bit of a rest [33]. If you do take them out at night, then is the time to soak them in denture cleaner. Clean them (with a toothbrush) at least once a day and after food if need be, but twice a day cleaning of your mouth much as when you had your own real teeth is still good. Some people like to clean their tongues as well with either the toothbrush or a tongue cleaner. I mention mouth care here because it is so often forgotten and so very important; not only does it keep your mouth in tip top condition (which it needs to be to

---

[29] Hazell T. *'Loss of Taste and Smell'* https://patient.info/ears-nose-throat-mouth/smell-and-taste-disorders Accessed 7th December 2023

[30] https://www.bhf.org.uk/informationsupport/support/healthy-living/healthy-eating/salt Accessed 7th December 2023

[31] https://patient.info/oral-dental-care/dentures Accessed 7th December 2023

[32] https://www.fixodent.co.uk/en-gb/advice-tips/living-with-dentures/cleaning-maintenance/can-you-sleep-in-your-dentures
Accessed 7th December 2023

[33] https://www.nhs.uk/conditions/dentures/ Accessed 7th December 2023

chew and taste the food you eat) but a clean mouth is a healthy one, or more to the point, an unclean mouth may be implicated in the development of a number of illnesses [34].

If your plate or dentures are not well fitting, go back to your dentist and get another pair/set that do. Ill-fitting false teeth cause sore areas which make eating painful and unpleasant, therefore inadvertently causing weight loss which is wanted in an elder population (unless of course it's deliberate, I'm talking about unplanned weight loss and subsequent malnutrition here) and to be avoided [35]. Also if they do not fit very well or cause soreness, take them out at night or when you sleep. Put them in as soon as you wake up and have cleaned your mouth though. A certain amount of soreness when one first gets them is to be expected as the gums heal and adjust to the new sensation of having plastic or metal in the mouth, this should pass though within a few weeks [36].

Loss of manual dexterity can be helped by using adapted equipment (your Occupational Therapist may well be able to advise), such as battery-operated toothbrushes, bigger handles that go over the toothbrush to make grasping easier and tube squeezers to get the cleaner or toothpaste from the tube.

Walking/ Mobility Aids

Let's deal now with adjuncts to getting about by which I mean walking sticks, walking frames, wheelchairs and mobility scooters. Firstly let me start by saying that not all folk as they get elderly will need any of these though statistically there is more immobility to be found in older folk than younger. And before you say "Well, duh! Obviously!", why is that so? Why does getting older bring with it difficulties in mobilising and moving about? Some of it is to do with a sedentary lifestyle [37], once people have retired there is less need to move about and that slowly increasing lack of movement leads to decreasing ability to get around [38]. Some of the immobility comes about as a result of disease processes such as diabetes or arthritis [39]. Muscle strength and form are lost, bones become brittle, the need for your brain to keep your body upright and stop you falling over becomes a little atrophied, coupled with the fact that your sight may not be as acute as it once was, or you are now taking tablets to lower your blood pressure which might make you dizzy anyway.

---

[34] Sambrook, J., *Oral Hygiene*, https://patient.info/oral-dental-care/toothache/oral-hygiene accessed 7th December 2023

[35] https://www.dentalhealth.org/caring-for-the-elderly Accessed 7th December 2023

[36] https://www.fixodent.co.uk/en-gb/advice-tips/for-new-denture-wearers/first-month-with-dentures Accessed 7th December 2023

[37] https://www.nhs.uk/live-well/exercise/exercise-as-you-get-older/ Accessed 10th December 2023

[38] https://www.nhs.uk/live-well/exercise/exercise-as-you-get-older/ Accessed 10th December 2023

[39] Godman, H., 'Two questions can reveal mobility problems in seniors', Harvard Health Blog, September 18th 2013, Sourced from health.harvard.edu/blog/two-questions-can-reveal-mobility-problems-in-seniors-201309186682 Accessed 10th December 2023

Whatever the cause, wherever you are in this scenario, things can always be make a bit better and a bit safer. Often the first time people realise that this is actually a 'problem' is when they get taken to hospital following a fall and get referred to the 'falls clinic', a clinic that is actually set up with the intention of lessening your risk of falling. Some of what they do involves assessing the medication you're taking to see if any of them are implicated, checking your sight, doing an ECG to see if there is any cardiac reason for dizziness [40]. You may see a physiotherapist who will assess your mobility and gait and who may advise you to use some form of equipment to help maintain your safety. They may also give you a set of exercises to do to strengthen your muscles [41].

Walking sticks

Walking sticks could be considered the starter kit of mobility aids, if you feel you need one you don't need to have supplied by a physiotherapist. Note that walking sticks are used by trail hikers on long distance paths who have no problem with them and do not believe that they necessarily make them look 'like an old person'. Their utility is recognised, it basically gives you another leg with which to walk and helps with balance on uneven ground [42]. Sticks can be bought online or in the high street, as part of a fashion statement, silver plated, with crystals, with Liberty patterns, made of fancy woods, with deer antlers for a handle. You name it, you can probably buy it. However, it does need to be of the right height for you. Imagine; a stick that is good for a person of 4' 11" is going to be no use to someone of 6' 5". To measure for the right size it is useful to have someone to help you and information on how to do this can be gained from a number of sources [43] though you can do it yourself if you have no willing volunteers. Ensure that you do get the right height as too high will put your shoulder out of alignment and too low will make you stoop. Ways of adjusting the height should be provided with the stick but are easily found online if not readily available. Some walking sticks come with little feet (3, a tripod or 4, a tetrapod/ quadruped) which increases the amount of stability the stick can give as it have a slightly wider base.

Learning to use the stick correctly is best learnt from a physiotherapist and certainly if you need two of them, there is a special technique. Also, for going up and down the stairs, education on the correct technique is important [44] so find one through your GP or pay for a private session.

---

[40] https://www.nhs.uk/conditions/falls/ Accessed 10th December 2023

[41] https://www.nhs.uk/conditions/falls/ Accessed 10th December 2023

[42] Kohl, J. '*5 Reasons to Use a Walking Stick*' on https://www.seekadventuresblog.com/5-reasons-to-use-a-walking-stick/ April 3rd 2018. Accessed 10th December 2023

[43] https://www.which.co.uk/later-life-care/home-care/out-and-about/choosing-a-walking-stick-a4q4h5y5g7w0 Accessed 10th December 2023

[44] https://www.which.co.uk/later-life-care/home-care/out-and-about/choosing-a-walking-stick-a4q4h5y5g7w0 Accessed 10th December 2023

Walking frames

Walking frames are the next step on from walking sticks and although you can probably buy a new or second hand one in a charity shop or online, they are best provided or at least advised by a physiotherapist. Their function is to provide a little more stability and to stop folk 'furniture walking' which is common in the more immobile population and also unsafe [45]. As with walking sticks the height is important but also, frames come in so many varieties; with two wheels, with no wheels, with three wheels and a brake (and sometimes a nifty little seat/ basket arrangement) known as a rollator, narrow gauge and 'gutter' frames. By the time mobility has deteriorated to such an extent that a walking frame is needed there needs to have been professional physiotherapy input as some of the options above are unsuitable to various conditions. There are implications in using the wrong one for the wrong purpose and I am not going to write about this much here, suffice to say that professional advice needs to be sought so that the person trying to get about with a little more stability doesn't fall over due to using the wrong frame or damage their shoulder joints by getting an inappropriate one.

Wheelchairs, again are mostly provided by the NHS once a physiotherapist has seen the person and deemed a wheelchair the best aid to mobility. They can also be bought privately and the usual rules apply…make sure it fits properly, is the right height (not only the height of the seat from the ground but also the length of the back of the wheelchair), is manoeuvrable, will fit through internal doors if it is for indoor use, ensure if it is to be self propelled that the wheels have an appropriate rim to allow you to generate forward motion. If you don't have the upper body strength to push it then there is not much point getting a self propelling one. These tend to have larger wheels so think about whether it will fit inside your home. If it is going to be used inside and outside, ensure it is robust enough to do so. Wheelchairs can also be rented or for impromptu or emergency use [46].

Wheelchairs

Wheelchairs can be customised to fit the user, so special cushions can be used or the height of head rests adjusted. The seat size is variable as we all come in different shapes and sizes so take care to ensure that you get one that is appropriate for you. It should not be a tight squeeze to get into it and neither should you be floating around like a lost pea in a saucepan, this thing is supposed to be giving you support. Be aware that sitting on your rear end for hours at a time is not good for the state of your skin and makes you liable to pressure damage. If you decided to go for a wheelchair, pay close attention to how the chair is going to do Its' best to prevent any pressure damage. If you are buying this equipment then ask copious questions and really drill down. I cannot emphasise enough how important this is and how avoiding a pressure sore is the main aim here.

---

[45] https://www.doctorpetty.com/furniture-walking-is-dangerous/ Accessed 10th December 2023

[46] https://www.redcross.org.uk/get-help/hire-a-wheelchair Accessed 10th December 2023

Mobility Scooters

Let me move on to mobility scooters, an aide to getting around in town, to do shopping or enable you to get further or visit your friends. I will also include motorised wheelchairs in this section too as from a legal and practical point of view, the two vehicles are similar in function. These are a privately purchased option so do your research and find something that will give you the best service and flexibility that you need. Things that need to be considered are; size - how big is it? Where are you going to store it when it's not in use? Will you be able to get it out the garden gate? Is it so supremely large that it's actually going to be an inconvenience in getting about and cause pedestrians some qualms when they see you bearing down on them. Much as you might want to cut a dash when you're out and about, it's pointless having something that is too big (or too small). With some scooters you may not use the road unless there is not a pavement or footway available so consider other path users.

How about charging the scooter, how will you do that? Where will that happen? Outside? What about the weather? Have you got a power point where you intend to park the scooter?

Legalities – will you need to register it? Note that only certain types of mobility scooters can be driven on the road and these need to be registered (though you don't need a licence [47] or insurance (although that is surely up to you and would be useful…you don't want to be sued by a pedestrian whose leg you broke by speeding down the precinct and you can be held liable for any injury you cause anyone else if you are the driver)). When you buy the vehicle, the vendor will be able to tell you if it needs to be registered and if you are in any doubt go on to the www.gov.uk site for clarification around this. You will become the Registered Keeper (the same as any vehicle) so if you're buying second hand, go onto the www.gov.uk web site and look for the forms to register the fact that it is now yours. Note also, Quad bikes need to be registered, MOT'd and taxed and the majority of them are not safe enough to use on the road as an alternative to a mobility scooter [48]. Sorry, they do sound like a lot of fun but really, not good for what we need here.

Mobility logistics – how will you actually get on to and off of the scooter? If it is going to be kept outside, can you actually get out of the door to get on to the vehicle? Do you have steps that need to be traversed either by you en route to the scooter or by the scooter itself? How is that going to happen? If the gate needs to be opened or closed behind you on the scooter, would that be able to happen or is it an impossibility?

Is it actually fit for purpose? These things are not cheap, the temptation is to buy the cheapest available…don't. Buy the best one for you. Bear in mind that it needs to bear your body weight in a safe and balanced manner, so some lightweight thing that leaves you top heavy and teetering is unsafe and makes you more liable to falling.

---

[47] https://www.gov.uk/mobility-scooters-and-powered-wheelchairs-rules Accessed 10th December 2023

[48] https://www.gov.uk/quad-bikes-the-rules Accessed 10th December 2023

Conclusion

OK, so that was a whistle stop tour of adjuncts and accessories to help out with some of the losses that can (note, they're not obligatory) occur as one gets older. Praise be that we live in an age where this knowledge and this stuff is available. Hope it's been helpful. As ever my advice is to get hold of the help you need as early as you can so that using it and doing so correctly becomes second nature and therefore helpful.

Useful websites and resources

https://www.abilitysuperstore.com is a company that sells a lot of equipment to help with independence and mobility, UK based, lots of useful links to charities and other agencies, a collection of 'how to' videos and a blog. Their postal address is The Mill, Gertrude Street, NELSON, BB9 8RS and phone number 0800 255 0498

https://www.allaboutvision.com is an online advice service about all things optical and to do with glasses, their articles provided are double verified and use recognised sources such as The Lancet. They do have affiliate links but nonetheless a useful resource, it'll give links to local optometrists and online glasses or contact lens providers.

https://www.amazon.co.uk I'm sure needs no introduction, as it is the world's market-place. Love it or loathe it, here it is.

https://www.dentalhealth.org/ is a charity 'dedicated to improving oral health' and it aims to do this by giving information and advice. They also have a list of accredited products. Postal address is Oral Health Foundation, Smile House, 2, East Union Street, RUGBY, Warwickshire, CV22 6AJ and their helpline contact number is 01788 539780

https://www.fixodent.co.uk is part of the Proctor and Gamble group and they sell denture fixative amongst other things. They have a small section for new denture wearers with little videos. Helpline is on 0800 731 3086

https://hearinghealthmatters.org is a general American catch all site for professionals involved in hearing loss care and for those actually experiencing it too. It aims to educate and provide "timely information".

https://www.hearingreview.com a "single-stop web site for the hearing industry", they report on innovations and research, products and practice.

https://journals.lww.com a private publishing company website dedicated to providing up to date information to its client group which is mostly within the broad remit of 'medicine and nursing'. Copious amounts of articles available.

https://leader.pubs.asha.org/ is a magazine for hearing and speech and language professionals (the American Speech-Language-Hearing Association). It is a news magazine and as such does not subject its material to peer review but gives a jump off point to investigate matters.

https://myhearingcenters.com is an American group that started small and is now growing, they provide testing and hearing aids and education for the patient, including some good, small explanations of hearing and hearing loss matters.

https://www.nhs.uk the website for the NHS with lots of information, how to find services you might need, check up on drugs you are taking, conditions you may have, there is also a video library dealing with more common conditions and advice on healthy living.

https://www.redcross.org.uk I think we probably all know of the Red Cross but may not be aware of the many services they offer. From hiring equipment, to help for refugees, to preparing for emergencies, in the UK and overseas. They are there for "Connecting human kindness with human crisis".

https://www.thcp.co.uk The Hearing Care Partnership is a private practice of audiology specialists that provide hearing aids and hearing treatment. Their web site details the variety of hearing aids that are available. They have affiliated practices throughout the country and a 'practice searcher' so you can find a local one. The phone number is 0800 5200 546

https://www.thelancet.com a long renowned medical journal, it has the reputation of being the *ne plus ultra* amongst such publications as it accepts only the best research to publish. It has a huge range of specific subjects and promotes the use of scientific research as an agent to prompt change.

https://www.walkingsticks.co.uk is a business with it's aim to 'ensure that all of our customers find a can that aids their mobility and looks good'. Based in London, they post to the UK and can be contacted on 020 7501 0591 and their contact address is Unit 6, Union Court, LONDON, SW4 6JP

https://www.which.co.uk/ a site devoted to learning which is the best version of practically everything that is for sale, they are a 'not for profit' group and fund their work through subscriptions, making them able to provide objective advice. It is part charity and part limited company. Their postal address is Which?, 3 Capital Quarter, Tyndall Street, CARDIFF, CF10 4BZ and their phone number is 020 7770 7000.

CHAPTER 3

Planning for unwanted eventualities and legalities

Next-of-kin/ inheritance/ wills

Your next-of-kin comes in two variations, that concerning who to call when you go into hospital and your legal next-of-kin. The medical/social next-of-kin is the person you would like kept up to date with your treatment and what is happening to you. If you don't nominate someone when you go into hospital, then it will be assumed to be either your spouse if still living or your nearest blood relative. The medical/social next-of-kin has no legal standing and cannot say what treatment you will or will not have [49] and it is purely a courtesy title so that someone is kept in the know on your behalf.

The next-of-kin by blood or marriage ties is a totally different matter, though still it does not carry with it any legal status [50] in Wales or England. If you want your next-of-kin to have any input into your care or treatment, if you become too unwell to say yourself then you need to appoint Lasting Power of Attorney to them. I will deal with this below. But for the moment we are dealing with inheritance and wills in this section so I'll just go to say the your next-of-kin from the legal point of view is your nearest living blood relative, or your spouse. Just let that sink in a bit, your nearest living relative. That might be the sibling you haven't spoken to for the last forty years after you fell out about something you have long forgotten. That might be your ne'er do well eldest child with the unfortunate tattoos, a drug habit and a plethora of unsavoury acquaintances. That might be a cousin you haven't seen since you were a child, who never phones or contacts you and who you happen to know holds political views in direct opposition to yours. At the risk of chucking a cliché in here, you can choose your friends, but you can't choose your family. Also worth mentioning here is that though your spouse is likely to be part of the general carve up should you die intestate, if you are not legally married or in a civil partnership at the time of death, they don't count as a spouse [51] [52]. Living together for fifty years still doesn't get them any legal standing...hey, it's not me that makes the rules, I'm just telling you. Also to let you know that if you have no living relatives of any sort (or even half relatives such as step aunts and uncles) then your goodies go to the Crown! [5] Of course, funding the Royal Family and the nation might be your idea of a good use of your wherewithal in which case, carry on, die intestate. If it's not....make a will! There are a heap of charities that can offer help in making a will and do a fabulous job taking care of or offering

---

[49] https://www.patients-association.org.uk/next-of-kin   Accessed 13th May 2021, checked 19th December 2023

[50] https://www.startpointlaw.co.uk/who-is-your-next-of-kin/ Accessed 13th May 2021, checked 19th December 2023

[51] https://www.thetimes.co.uk/money-mentor/answer/live-in-partner-property-rights/ 'Would a live-in partner have rights to my property?', updated July 29, 2020, accessed 14th May 2021, checked 19th December 2023

[52] https://www.citizensadvice.org.uk/family/death-and-wills/who-can-inherit-if-there-is-no-will-the-rules-of-intestacy/ Accessed 14th May 2021, checked 19th December 2023

support to a cause dear to your heart...have a look online at your specific favourite cause or try https://www.willaid.org.uk.

So if you pop your clogs without writing a will then after a bit of too-ing and fro-ing, solicitors and other legal advisors, your next-of-kin will get your estate. Therefore my Dahlinks, make a will! It's really easy, any solicitor can draft it for you, they'll send you the rough copy and if you are in agreement and it shares it all out as you want it to be done, then you just get it signed (either in the solicitor's office or they can come to you if mobility is a problem). Scrappy bits of paper with your last wishes, unwitnessed by anybody but the beneficiaries (those that are going to benefit from your will and get money, property or goods [53]) do not count. A legal will needs to be witnessed by two independent people, neither of whom can be the beneficiaries or their marriage partner. Do this properly. If you can't afford to see a solicitor about it, lots of charities do a sort of deal whereby they'll help you draft it, see my above reference for willaid. You can also get a form from stationers which allow you to draw up your own will and arrange for two independent people to witness it. This is not a morbid thing, this is a caring act to do, a sort of last tidy up! Your family and friends will have enough to do and will be utterly distraught, the last thing they're going to need is some legal shenanigans about who gets what. And make no mistake, folk get very emotional about wills and inheritance, you don't want to provoke that sort of upset (or maybe you do but what's the point? You won't be there to see it. Whilst I'm on this subject...if you want to 'disinherit' (ie. not leave money or goods to) a member of your family who would normally expect to inherit something because you don't like them, they've irritated you beyond measure, ignored your wishes, behaved in a reprehensible manner or for whatever reason, you can merely not include them in your will but if it is going to be a huge and bitterly disappointing surprise for them, it might be kinder to add an addendum to the will explain your reason why. You don't have to do this. It just strikes me as polite. And saves other people worrying if undue pressure was put on you to sign something that you really didn't want to sign).

Power of Attorney and Capacity assessments

Another form you might want to think about completing and making legal and valid is that of Lasting Power of Attorney. All the social care agencies and all the health agencies in the UK will turn heaven and earth to allow you to do what you want when you're unwell. They will support you in your decision to not have treatment and to go home even if they think it is really not wise. They will happily wave you goodbye as you head off into the sunset to continue living in what they consider to be utter squalor with no central heating or cooking facilities apart from one gas ring. Really, the whole system is set up to allow you to live the life you want with no interference from anybody (unless of course you are a danger to other people or yourself and even then the amount of forms and proforma to go through are phenomenal and involve more than one professional). The NHS website that deals with capacity and assessments sums it all up neatly:

---

[53] https://www.moneyadviceservice.org.uk/en/articles/diy-wills-what-you-need-to-know Accessed 14th May 2021, checked 19th December 2023

"All adults are presumed to have sufficient capacity to decide on their own medical treatment, unless there's significant evidence to suggest otherwise." [54]

So...all this is fine until you become unable to say what it is you'd like (because you've had a stroke which has left you incapacitated and unable to put thoughts together logically or you have become delirious (because you've got an infection that has altered your perception of reality) or you have dementia). Or you cannot make a decision as you can't retain the information for long enough. Or your process of reasoning has taken a battering and you can't weigh up the pros and cons effectively [55]. In other words, you do not have 'capacity' to make a sensible, reasoned decision taking into account all the risks that might be inherent in the situation. And it is that latter point that is the nub of this decision. You need to be able to take account of and accept the risks and you need to be able to communicate the same [8]. If you are mentally no longer in a position to do that, if you don't realise that what you want to do has risks then after a long and proper assessment....you are deemed to 'lack capacity'. This is not a decision that is set in tablets of stone and forever. If someone is assessed as lacking capacity, but then say, three months later is much better and expresses an awareness of risk and appears more lucid then a reassessment of capacity will be done and perhaps (and I have seen this occur) the initial decision of 'lack of capacity' will be reversed and the patient can do what they like.

Being assessed for capacity is nothing to be scared of, the staff involved in this decision take it very seriously. It is not a decision that is made 'on the hoof', rather it is an undertaking that takes time and research. It is governed by the Mental Capacity Act 2005 [56] so set up in legislation to protect us all as far as it can. Some agencies employ a specific person to complete the capacity assessments, one who has undergone training and perhaps has other experience to help in this matter. Even if you are deemed not to have capacity, the staff dealing with you are professionally and legally bound to do the least restrictive thing for you every time and to act in your best interests. But of course, your best interests may not be what you want. You may have decided opinions about feeding towards the end of life or whether you want to go home even if it will be difficult vs going into a care home.

If therefore, you are deemed to lack capacity, your Lasting Power of Attorney for health and welfare is able to make decisions for you based on what they know of your wishes (and this is not the same as the 'Living Will' with which I will deal later). Lasting Power of Attorney is divided into two areas and it is possible to have a different person named for each area. One for health and welfare and the other for property and financial affairs [57]. The person (s) you appoint as your Attorney does/do not need to be a relative, it can be someone completely unrelated to you. It does

---

[54] https://www.nhs.uk/conditions/consent-to-treatment/capacity Accessed 14th May 2021, checked 19th December 2023

[55] https://www.mentalhealth.org.uk/explore-mental-health/a-z-topics/mental-capacity Accessed 14th May 2021, checked 19th December 2023

[56] https://www.legislation.gov.uk/ukpga/2005/9/contents gives the Act in all it's fine detail. Checked 19th December 2023

[57] https://www.gov.uk/power-of-attorney Accessed 14th May 2021, checked 19th December 2023

need to be someone that you trust, implicitly. So have a good think about this, who would you want to speak for you if you were not able? Who would you want to make important decisions about what happens if you are so ill you can no longer talk for yourself? I must mention here that if you do not trust family members to do the best for you, make somebody else your Attorney. Those of us that have nobody that we trust enough with this weighty decision making, can make your solicitor your Power of Attorney as well, though giving them a good understanding of where you stand and what your views are about extension of life at any cost would be useful. For more detailed information, clearly put, on this matter the www.gov.uk [58] is a good resource and tells you who can or cannot act for you, when LPA can be rescinded and other details. It also tells you how to go about completing this process, how much it costs, how long it takes (at least four weeks wait before application of paperwork and granting of LPA). Please bear in mind that this is a legal document, if the person acting as your LPA needs to step in as you've lost capacity, the staff that are leading decision making processes will want to see the paperwork. Again scraps of paper scribbled out on the kitchen table will not cut the mustard and are not worth the paper they're scrawled on.

The person with Lasting Power of Attorney for health and welfare is unable to act on your behalf and the whole thing does not come into force unless and until you lose capacity. So if the rest of your days are spent with a complete set of marbles and the ability to communicate such, it'll never come into action. It's worth having though because…who knows what's going to happen.

And I deal with this in detail because if you don't have someone appointed as having Power of Attorney for you, who knows your wishes, then the people making the decisions about your treatment and what will happen to you in the future are the Nurses and the Social Workers who don't really know you. They will decide if you need to go into a home, they will decide which home (realistically it'll be the first one with a bed available) and they will do all of this in your 'best interest', which of course may not be what you want at all.

Living Will/ Advance Decision/ Advance Directive of Refusal of Treatment

We've all heard of the idea of a 'living will', a document that will convey our wishes concerning our medical treatment if we are unable to do so (as we've had a stroke or have been left in a coma by having a car accident or any of a number of things that can leave us incapacitated) and certainly this is an action worth considering. It is also known as an 'Advance Decision' is a decision about our care and treatment made in advance, or an 'Advance Directive of Refusal of Treatment'. There is an extremely thorough information sheet available from Age UK [59] that runs to 72 pages and

---

[58] https://www.gov.uk/power-of-attorney Accessed 14th May 2021

[59] https://www.ageuk.org.uk/globalassets/age-uk/documents/factsheets/fs72_advance_decisions_advance_statements_and_living_wills_fcs.pdf?dtrk=true Accessed 14th May 2021, checked 19th December 2023

again, information can also be found from various agencies or downloaded from online sources [60] [61] [62] [63].

For it to have validity, you need to be *compus mentis* when you write it or have it written for you [1], it has to be in writing, signed by you, witnessed (by someone who is not closely connected with you or has day to day dealing involved in your care…you don't want accusations of pressure being put upon you by other people to occur at a later date if folk don't agree with your advance decision) and if you are absolutely vehement and sure that this is what you want and if some of the treatment you are refusing in advance may cost you your life, you have to add in a sentence that you are aware of that. So, a scrappy bit of paper on the kitchen table does not count and neither does your son saying 'Oh I know Dad would hate that'. Don't forget that medical professionals are trying to do the best for you and to save your life on the usual assumption that most folks want to live. Unless you tell them otherwise through a thoroughly legal form, they will not take anyone else's say so. And it does really help them to know that there are treatments that you wouldn't countenance, plus it can help your family if you become very ill…nobody needs to make a decision in the heat of the moment for which they may later regret or feel subsequent guilt [64]. In England and Wales at the time of writing, an adequately prepared Advanced Directive is enough to direct the medical team with giving or withholding treatment with legal backup, the laws in the devolved countries vary slightly but the upshot is that if a properly filled out Advance Directive is in place then medics will do their best to abide by your wishes and desires [65].

The variety of treatments that you may want to consider including in your Advance Directive are such things as:- do you want to have cardiopulmonary resuscitation if you have a cardiac or respiratory arrest? Would feeding via a tube to keep you alive be a procedure you would want? If whilst you're unwell with whatever took you into hospital and then you develop a secondary illness, would you want that illness treated (for instance, if you went into hospital with a profound stroke and then developed pneumonia, would you want the pneumonia treated?)? If you had profound and lasting brain damage would you want your life to be saved at all costs? Would you want to be alive on a ventilator whilst in a coma or would you rather that nature be allowed to take its course? Would you want intravenous fluids or nutrition that is not via the usual route of the stomach? [66] These are all questions that bear thinking about lest you find yourself in an unhappy

---

[60] https://www.nhs.uk/conditions/end-of-life-care/advance-decision-to-refuse-treatment/ Accessed 14th May 2021, checked 19th December 2023

[61] https://www.legalwills.co.uk/advance_directives Accessed 14th May 2021, checked 19th December 2023

[62] https://patient.info/doctor/advance-care-planning Accessed 14th May 2021, checked 19th December 2023

[63] https://www.alzheimers.org.uk/get-support/legal-financial/download-free-template-advance-decision-form Accessed 14th May 2021, checked 19th December 2023

[64] www.solicitorsforolderpeoplescotland.co.uk/guides/Guide-to-Advance-Directives.pdf Accessed 14th May 2021, checked 19th December 2023

[65] https://compassionindying.org.uk/how-we-can-help/planning-ahead/ Accessed 15th May 2021, checked 19th December 2023

[66] https://patient.info/doctor/advance-care-planning Accessed 15th May 2021, checked 19th December 2023

position of not being able to say what you'd like to be done and what are your preferences. Providing the forms are legally robust, the medical team in charge of your care will bow to your decision that you have made in advance. Because, here's the thing...we none of us know how our end will come. We hope it will be calm and an ordered forward motion towards a peaceful end... but it might not be, and in case of that, isn't it better to have thought about what you do or do not want?

There are certain things that you can't legally refuse. Analgesia, basic care (ie. keeping you clean and washed and in clean clothes and preventing any sores erupting as a result of pressure damage) [67] and food and drink by mouth. And you may not ask the team to do anything illegal for you (such as euthanasia) or ask for medical treatment that your consultant and her team think inappropriate (no-one is likely to object to aromatherapy or massage or reiki if you're paying for it, this clause is here to prevent you spending heaps of NHS money on treatments that are unlikely to be of any use whatsoever). You cannot refuse treatment for a mental health issue either [9].

An Advance Decision of Refusal of Treatment is legal as long as it's properly signed and witnessed, you had mental capacity when you had it drawn up (or wrote it down yourself) and it applies to the situation. Bear in mind also that if after signing it, you say anything that indicates you've changed your mind, the medical team will always go for the life sustaining option. They are legally and professionally bound to do so. So, if you do change your mind, just tell them [68].

Living wills (Advance Decision, Advance Directive) differ from Advance Statements which are much less formal but deal with much more concerning your likes and dislikes, what foods you prefer, what you will or will not eat, who you want to visit you if you become unwell, whether you prefer to have baths or showers or what sort of clothes you like to wear, what religion you are and whether you'd like spiritual sustenance from coreligionists. It can also include who will take care of your pets if you're ill, whether you'd prefer to be looked after at home or in a nursing home or a hospice if appropriate [69]. All this is the social stuff that ensures you are in the happiest state of mind as possible as things are being done for you in the way that you prefer. Please bear in mind with the above subjects that though I am talking mostly about end of life care, you do not need to wait until you've been given a terminal diagnosis or you feel the end is nigh to get this done. Anytime is good and in all honesty, better to have such things in place and never need to invoke them than find yourself in the position of wishing to goodness you had.

---

[67] https://patient.info/doctor/advance-care-planning Accessed 15th May 2021, checked 19th December 2023

[68] https://www.ageuk.org.uk/globalassets/age-uk/documents/factsheets/fs72_advance_decisions_advance_statements_and_living_wills_fcs.pdf Accessed 15th May 2021, checked 19th December 2023

[69] https://www.nhs.uk/conditions/end-of-life-care/advance-statement/ Accessed 15th May 2021, checked 19th December 2023

Going into hospital and procedures whilst in there

Very often and early on in the stay of someone in hospital the team may get together with the patient's next-of-kin to tell them the basic idea of what is happening, what usually happens, potential problems that may arise, how the team see that patient's likely journey through hospital. This may not involve all the members of the teams of people looking after the patient, as early on it is possible that not all members of the team have been identified. It may not be realised at this point that SaLT need to be involved for example or the Dietician. This sort of less formal meeting will usually happen within the first two weeks of a patient coming into hospital and will in no way negate the need for an MDT if one is called for later. It is often more likely with conditions that follow a set pathway of treatment (such as a stroke or a heart attack) and is more than likely not to involve the patient as they're laying in bed having treatment and hopefully getting better.

That may be the total experience you or your next-of-kin have with meeting the medical team if you go into hospital for whatever reason, make a fantastic recovery, are hale and hearty and good to go, being discharged home will not be problematic at all. At some point the doctors will give you a time they think you'll go home and let you know that they've finished your treatment. You may need to wait for any medication to take home with you and if you can't arrange transport or someone to collect you and going home on a bus or paying for a taxi isn't feasible, then you may have to wait for hospital transport as well. Be that said, basically if you're fit and well then you'll go home with nothing more than logistics problems of how to get there.

If it transpires that you may need a little input from carers at home and that apart from that discharge is without problems then this may be sorted out fairly easily. I'll deal with Social Workers and their role in Chapter 4 but suffice it to say here that you will likely need referral to one and they can arrange carers. If that is all that is needed then again, good to go as soon as the logistics have been sorted out.

Multi-disciplinary team meetings

If however, you have long lasting difficulties as a result of the condition that brought you into hospital, or that developed once you were there and going home is not going to be an easy option, then the staff will ask for a Multi-Disciplinary Team meeting (an 'MDT' for short). An MDT does not have to happen in hospital but this may be the first time you have come across the term and the format so I'll treat it as though it were. This is a getting together of all the members of the health team, anyone at all that is having regular input into your care (see Chapter 4 which deals with all these people that you may meet). A good explanation of best practice for MDT's is found on the NHS website, just search under the heading of "Making it happen: Multi-disciplinary team (MDT) working". Either you or someone you assign (usually your next-of-kin) will also be present. Never forget that all these people are here to help you get the best possible out of your life, they have no interest in keeping anything secret...what they want is for you and your family and friends to be assured that what is happening is the appropriate and best treatment for you. Having gathered everyone together, the usual format is for someone of the professions to act as chairperson, often the doctor who is present or sometimes the nurse. In an ideal world everyone would have a chance to say their piece. The whole point of this meeting is to explain in the open how the treatment is going, what the possible best result will be and how the 'team' and the patient will work to get there. This is your chance to ask questions about your future and for your next-of-kin to also understand what is happening. People don't want to make life difficult for you but there are times when going home to how you were prior to this admission and living the life you led then, are just not feasible. And if that is the case or is a very likely scenario, then the team are in the unenviable position of having to tell you this, something you do not want to hear, something that will possibly upset you, something that you will not want to come to terms with. But remember, the whole point of treatment in hospital is to get you as well as you can be and to do nothing without your consent. So whilst you may not want to hear this news, they are not telling you for the sheer fun of it. They really think that's how it is. And whilst you've never been in this position before, they have looked after a lot of people who have had it, they have the experience.

Say for instance that you require care from carers in the night. Some authorities provided such services, many don't. And if you live in an area where these are not provided, there are few options left to you. You could pay someone privately to be a night-time carer, you could go and live with a friend or relative and get them to be your carer at night (remember here that care usually involves hands on care of the body, cleaning up or keeping clean so is not a calling for everyone). Failing that, the only other option is going into a residential home. And that is the sort of news that few people want to hear. But, try as you might, it is not going to go away. Moreover once you are medically fit to leave, the consultant in charge of your care or their team are happy that you are fit to leave and the MDT are content that you are fit to leave your time in hospital then becomes a Delayed Transfer of Care (the pejorative term 'bed blocker' should never sully your ears and if it does report the offender to their superior for disciplinary action (that is my personal advice not my professional stance but it is a phrase I hate as it demeans patients and makes them the 'villain' [70]), it is a wording that needs swift eradication from the public arena). So, the idea of presenting your options to you is to allow you to come to terms with them and to figure out what is the best in this situation. At this point, the meeting and you may well come to the decision that residential care would be the best place to meet your needs and your next-of-kin or friends or whoever is acting on your behalf would be asked to identify the institution you/they would prefer. Now, places in residential homes are not available willy nilly, often there will be a wait so in the interim, you may well be placed somewhere that does have a bed. This is an 'interim' bed, only temporary whilst you're waiting. Needs must and all that...

---

[70] Excellent article here on this subject https://theguardian.com/healthcare-network/2016/aug/30/bed-blockers-older-people-language-health-service checked 19th December 2023

Decisions on residential vs nursing homes

Usually, the nurses on the ward will complete what is known as a Nursing Needs Assessment if it looks likely that the patient will not be able to safely go home without care. This will assess the patient in several criteria and give occasion for any needs to be flagged up. They will use their knowledge of the patient and will refer to the notes that have been made over the time the patient has been in hospital by nurses, doctors, all the members of the Multi-Disciplinary Team and will be able to pinpoint using this tool, if nursing care is needed.

Supposing however that going home, even with carers is not feasible, then one will need to go into some form of residential care home. The following question from that decision is…would nursing or residential care be more appropriate? Places that offer nursing care are different in some ways from places that are purely residential and the main difference being, a nurse is always on duty in the former [71]. Now, this makes a difference to what sort of care can be provided. If one needs help with getting washed and dressed, moving about and meals provided, this comes under the remit of a residential care home. They are set up to look after (but not 'nurse', big distinction) folk who have needs that could potentially be met inside their own home but usually for logistical reasons cannot be. This would be things such as needing care at night, needing someone to provide cooked food (Social Service carers do not do cooking other than opening a packet meal and putting it in a microwave) or needing help getting washed and dressed and dealing with mobility issues [72]. In these places, care is given by non-nursing staff and depending on the nature of the establishment, those staff may be highly trained or otherwise. Any institution has to meet stringent regulations, these include staff training but they are not nurses and one need not expect them to be. If a resident should need nursing care temporarily, then the usual practice would be to get the District Nurse involved though if the need turned out to be permanent then moving from residential to nursing care may be more appropriate

Nursing homes provide nursing care that is a little more complex than could be met by a residential care home [73] That would include such actions as feeding someone by a tube that goes down the nose and into the stomach, giving drugs via a special port inserted underneath the patient's skin, giving regular wound care (*ad hoc* wound care in a residential home would be given by District/ Community Nurses but if this is a long standing or permanent wound then nursing care will be needed) or looking after someone who is very prone to seizures and therefore at risk of hurting themselves. And it will come as no surprise I'm sure, that the cost of staying in a nursing home is greater than that of staying in a residential home. As I write this the average cost of a week in a

---

[71] https://www.carehome.co.uk/ will provide greater details on this and they also give reviews of the various establishments throughout the country. Accessed 19th May 2021, checked 19th December 2023

[72] https://www.trustedcare.co.uk/help-and-advice/difference-care-home-nursing-home Accessed 19th December 2023

[73] https://www.nhs.uk/conditions/social-care-and-support-guide/care-services-equipment-and-care-homes/care-homes Accessed 19th May 2021, checked 19th December 2023

residential care home is approx. £800 a week and a nursing home is more [74]. Obviously given the potential conditions that may have to be met, the need to more equipment and the level of expertise of the staff, it will involve greater outlay by the institution itself.

If one needs to go to a nursing home for nursing care then the state will contribute towards the cost of the nursing component of the fees set by the institution. There are two levels of support and this is paid directly to the nursing home. There is also a form of funding called Continuing Health Care funding which meets the nursing part of the cost of a nursing home completely though not the 'hotel' part of the fees. These are expected to be met by the patient or from the patient's assets. If there are not enough assets (the current rate in England and Northern Ireland is having assets over £23,250, in Wales assets over £50,000, in Scotland that figure is £28,750 [75]) then the local authority will meet some of that cost. I say thank goodness for Social Workers who know how all this stuff works.

The recognition of nursing needs or the non recognition of them can be a contentious business for reasons around funding decisions. A

> "...healthcare need..., in general terms it can be said that such a need is one related
>
> to the treatment, control or prevention of a disease, illness, injury or disability, and
>
> the care or aftercare of a person with these needs..." [76]

And it is these sort of needs that count as 'nursing'. A social care need is defined as being focused on the normal activities of daily living such as social interaction and maintaining independence, just the normal everyday stuff of living. But how do you know if it is a nursing home or a residential care home that is needed? If you are completely self-funding and you do not need nursing care then you could choose to go to whichever residential place you want to, a residential care home or a nursing home, whichever you fancy the look of most and whoever is happy to have you. But if you do have recognised nursing needs then you can only be looked after in a registered nursing home.

The method of discerning if a nursing or residential home is needed is an assessment called a Continuing Healthcare Decision Support Tool, an unwieldy document that runs to 37 pages [77]. It calls for evidence to support the identified need for nursing or social care in a total of eleven (sometimes twelve) domains including behaviour, cognition, mobility, nutrition and altered states of consciousness. In each individual domain, evidence is provided to garner a 'score' of a range of needs, from 'No Needs' to 'Priority'. This assessment is completed at a group meeting, in which all

---

[74] https://www.nhs.uk/conditions/social-care-and-support-guide/care-services-equipment-and-care-homes/care-homes Accessed 19th May 2021, checked 19th December 2023

[75] https://www.theguardian.com/society/2023/oct/17/uk-care-homes-pay-fees-residential-care Accessed 19th December 2023

[76] https://caretobedifferent.co.uk/establishing-a-primary-health-care-need/ Accessed 19th December 2023

[77] https://www.gov.uk/government/publications/nhs-continuing-healthcare-decision-support-tool Accessed 20th May 2021, checked 19th December 2023

the relevant people involved in the patient's care and the patient and the patient's next-of-kin and/ or LPA are present. If some of the professionals are unable to attend then they will submit a report in anticipation. The patient's Social Worker will also be present. The process is usually led by a senior ward nurse (it doesn't have to be a senior nurse, in fact anyone could do the assessment, it's just that the training to do it well and properly isn't usually offered to more junior nurses as they have so much else to be trained in) in concert with all the other members of the MDT. Why a nurse? This is because nurses are the one professional group that are with the person during their hospital stay 24/7. They will know if care is needed at night, they will have an idea of how often the patient has seizures if that is relevant, they will know how often a feeding pump needs to be checked and how often wounds will need to be assessed. If pain management or end-of-life care is necessary then it is not a given that a nursing home is needed. End-of-life care can be managed in a residential home with support from District /Community Nurses and the GP much the same as if the patient was at home. But of course, in this decision input is needed from all the other professionals as well, the Physiotherapist and the Occupational Therapist, possibly the Dietician and the Speech and Language therapist.

Given that the decision of the assessment can result in a patient or their family either paying or not paying anything up to £500 a week extra, you can imagine the emotional attachment to the result and this is why the decision will be made in 'the light of day' with all members of the team present and either the patient or the patient's assigned representative. And this can be done quite imaginatively even if the patient's representative cannot themselves get to the meeting. The marvels of modern communication technology mean meetings can be attended by phone or computer screen. So, everyone will get their chance to say what they need to concerning the physical, mental and behavioural abilities and potential problems experienced by the patient. Plans of care may be addressed by some of the team members and all this occurs whilst the decision-making form is being filled out. This is to ensure that everyone is in agreement with the decision and the rationale underlying the decision. Ultimately, somebody needs to sign that document to say that in their professional opinion the patient needs or does not need nursing care funding, so you can see why it is important that everyone is aware of the decision made and why. I usually find when taking part in this process that relatives are happy to have been included in the process and get to understand why the ultimate decision is made. However, as I said above, understandings on what constitutes nursing and what constitutes social care are sometimes difficult and can be contentious. Bear in mind also that the evidence presented to back up the decisions made will be related to that admission for the patient, what they're like at home or previous to this hospital admission is not factored in because there is no evidence to support that.

Once the documentation has been completed and the meeting concluded, the nurse that led the meeting will then send the paperwork and all of the supporting evidence to the local Clinical Commission Group or a panel appointed by them to ratify or challenge [78]. The CCG will go over the paperwork and the evidence provided with a fine-toothed comb ensuring that this really is the

---

[78] https://www.porterdodson.co.uk/blog/nhs-continuing-healthcare-assessment-process Accessed 20th May 2021, checked 19th December 2023

correct decision. It can take a week or so for the final decision to be reached. If the DST meeting concludes that the patient is not eligible for continuing funded nursing care then the patient or the patient's family are liable for the nursing content of the care home fees minus a bit that the NHS pay. As I write this the amount the NHS pay to nursing homes for care is £187.60 or there is higher rate of £258.08 [79] although there are variations in amounts in devolved countries. There is of course an appeal process. If the DST concludes that the patient does meet the criteria for NHS Continuing Healthcare funding then the full amount of the nursing part of the bill is paid for by the NHS [80].

Conclusion

Get it done and get it done before you need it in the hope that you never will. I could've gone into much greater detail here but why? It's enough that you get the gist of this and are aware that such forms and legalities need attending to earlier rather than rue the fact that it's now too late to do anything about it.

Useful websites and resources

https://www.ageuk.org.uk/ A charity dedicated to helping and speaking out for the older portion of society, those without anyone else to help them. They have local groups that can supply help and advice and of course run charity shops throughout the UK.

https://www.alzheimers.org.uk/ A charity providing information, factsheets, selling dementia friendly items and has links to various support services. Postal address is Alzheimer's Society, 43-44 Crutched Friars, LONDON, EC3N 2AE and their phone number is 0330 333 0804

https://caretobedifferent.co.uk/ Care to be Different are a privately owned group who give detailed information regarding navigating a way through the Continuing Healthcare Funding process. Their postal address is The Copper Room, Deva City Office Park, Trinity Way, SALFORD, M3 7BG. They have a lot of articles of information and sell books and guides to help you through the process, including how to choose a care home, what to look for and the questions to ask. Although initially set up as a voluntary resource it is now owned by a company of solicitors who have expertise in this matter. Nonetheless the free information is valuable and helpful and there is no need to sign up to deal with a solicitor if you don't want to or have no need to do so.

https://www.citizensadvice.org.uk/ A registered charity with a web site that will lead you specifically to the nation in which you require information before dealing with it. Helpful because things do differ between devolved nations. Their remit is pretty wide and covers money, debt, law,

---

[79] https://www.gov.uk/government/news/nhs-funded-nursing-care-rate-to-increase Accessed 20th May 2021, checked 19th December 2023

[80] https://www.elder.org/nhs-continuing-healthcare-funding/#how-much-is-continuinh-healthcare-funding Accessed 20th May 2021, checked 19th December 2023

health, benefits, housing. There is an advice link service, a free phone call on 0800 702 2020, available 09:00 hrs to 17:00 hrs. Postal address is Citizen's Advice, 3rd Floor North, 200, Aldersgate, LONDON, EC1A 4HD

https://compassionindying.org.uk/ Set up to help people with an information line and very much focused on helping people fill out their Advance Decisions, their aim is to help plan for eventualities. Postal address is 181, Oxford Street, LONDON, W1D 2JT and their phone number is 0800 999 2434

https://www.gov.uk is a treasure trove of information though it isn't particularly attractively presented. Nonetheless, a good trawl through this website can turn up all sorts of interesting things. Here I've given the link to the bit about Power of Attorney though there's lots more to discover if you have a taste for the legal minutiae of the country.

https://www.hospiceuk.org/ A charity that works "…for the benefit of people affected by death and dying…"deals with all things hospice including a useful hospice finder, support for those dealing with bereavement, educational material. Their address is Hospice UK, 34-44 Britannia Street, LONDON, WC1X 9JG

https://www.kingsfund.org.uk/about-us The King's Fund is a charitable organisation that commissions and funds research into the health sector in England. They provide scholarly articles and blogs and run educational events and have a series of useful and accessible audio and visual shorts to explain various elements in the care system. Postal address is The King's Fund, 11-13, Cavendish Square, LONDON, W1G 0AN and their telephone number is 020 7307 2400

https://www.legalwills.co.uk/advance_directives An alternative to a face-to-face solicitor, all done online, and also allows you to name 'keyholders' who can access your information given certain criteria (set by you). The service costs of course but less than a solicitor's visit in person.

https://www.legislation.gov.uk/ 'The Official Home of Revised Enacted UK Legislation' from 1267 onwards. If it's on the statute books, if it's a current act of law, it'll be here somewhere.

https://www.macmillan.org.uk A charity that supports people with cancer, offering support financially, emotionally and with physical matters. Their support line is on 0808 808 00 00 and their postal address is Macmillan Cancer Support, 89, Albert Embankment, LONDON, SE1 7UQ.

https://www.mariecurie.org.uk Initially set up as a charity to help those with cancer it has widened it's remit to include all persons with terminal illnesses, runs hospices and funds research. They provide (resources permitting) nursing at home as well. Postal address is Marie Curie, 89, Albert Embankment, LONDON, SE1 7TP and the helpline is reached on 0800 920 2309

https://www.mentalhealth.org.uk/ This is a charity devoted to increasing awareness of mental health issues and funding research into such however they are not a service provider. They do have links though for people in crisis to reach for help and support. Lots of information about mental health and for personal actions around mental health maintenance.

https://www.moneyhelper.org.uk/en   A group set up by the government to help people manage their money, keep out of or minimise debt, budget, plan pension and there is a range of tools and calculators available to help work stuff out. Twenty four hour available helpline is on 0800 138 7777, postal address is The Money Advice Service, 120, Holborn, LONDON, EC1N 2TD

https://www.nhs.uk/   The website for the NHS with lots of information, how to find services you might need, check up on drugs you are taking, conditions you may have, there is also a video library dealing with more common conditions and advice on healthy living.

https://patient.info/ Originally a start up by two GP's this web resource has considerably expanded and is now part of EMIS healthcare, a health IT provider. The articles provided are by registered professionals and the site gives leaflets on lots of conditions. A useful resource. Their registered office is at Fulford Grange, Micklefield Lane, Rawdon, LEEDS, LS19 6BA.

https://www.patients-association.org.uk/ This is a registered charity whose focus is to campaign for better social and health care for patients and who liaise with the government at times. If you're feeling a bit lost in the system, these are the folk that can help you make sense of it and suggest alternative paths to follow. Note that they do not give legal or medical advice though. Helpline is 0800 345 7115 and their postal address is P Block, Northwick Park Hospital, THE North west Hospitals NHS Trust, Watford Road, HARROW, Middlesex, HA1 3UJ

CHAPTER 4

Professional and Specialist help that can make life easier

This chapter deals with the various professionals that you may well meet or want to access to help you out. I give a short description of their role and detail how to access them. I cannot sing the praises of my fellow professionals sufficiently. All of these people are interested in keeping you as well as possible, as active as possible, in your own home or environment of choice for as long as possible, as independent as possible. And all of them together provide a team with expertise second to none. Make use of their expertise if you need it.

The GP

Your General Practitioner is there to treat common illnesses that can be managed at home, especially the chronic ones and to spot any potential need for referral onwards to specialist services [81] so they act as a gatekeeper. They spend a large amount of their time seeing patients (of all ages and all states of health) individually in the surgery, a bit of time liaising with fellow professionals and referring people to consultants and in rural areas they may well be responsible for managing a community hospital as well. They may also do 'home visits'. It is a busy and long day for most GP's. The typical case load of patients for whom they are responsible is about 1800 [82] though that differs depending on locality and population density with some areas being very short of enough GP's to adequately meet service needs [83]. They spend an extra three years after basic doctor training in hospital posts specifically tailored to help them as GP's, such as Paediatrics, Obstetrics, Psychiatry, Dermatology, ENT...they won't necessarily do all of these but there will be a selection of useful posts to help them with their clinical knowledge in the field [84]. They will also be leading on government initiatives on local levels, things such as management of hypertension or ensuring that all people in certain criteria get necessary tests. Doctors are attracted to this as a vocation because there is a huge variety of work, the general medical knowledge they need to know and the number of patients they get to see [85]. One of the reasons they leave is due to stress, working very long hours with not enough time to adequately deal with patients and their ailments

---

[81] https://www.healthcareers.nhs.uk/explore-roles/doctors/roles-doctors/general-practitioner Accessed 18th December 2023

[82] https://www.healthcareers.nhs.uk/explore-roles/doctors/roles-doctors/general-practitioner Accessed 18th December 2023

[83] https://www.bbc.co.uk/news/health-46912055 Accessed 6th July 2021, checked 18th December 2023

[84] https://gprecruitment.hee.nhs.uk/Recruitment/Training Accessed 6th July 2021, checked 18th December 2023

[85] https://www.gponline.com/top-ten-reasons-nhs-gp/article/1373802 Accessed 6th July 2021, checked 18th December 2023

and the huge amount of the work they have to do [86]. If you want to help them to help you, make the most of your visit by having all the information to hand before you go in. They will want a timeline of the reason you are visiting (when the problem started, how long has it been going on, have you tried anything to remedy it? What are the symptoms you are experiencing?) and they've got on average ten minutes to hear what you have to say and think about appropriate treatment or referral. Please do not leave what you have really come to see them about until you are going out of the door. Be plain speaking, tell it like it is, don't be unnecessarily coy, help them to help you as much as you can. You don't need to know the medical words, the common language will do but don't use offensive language either. These are highly trained and skilled people with a huge amount of knowledge…but they are not clairvoyant and the more relevant information you can give, the better a picture they can build up.

Speech and Language Therapist

I wish this profession would tweak their name to include the all-important information that they also assess and deal with people that have a poor or incompetent swallow [87]. This mostly brings a Speech and Language Therapist (SaLT) into contact with folk when they are in hospital. So let me deal with swallowing first and we'll go onto the actual speech and language bit in a minute.

The ability to swallow food and fluids is a subtle bodily skill that we completely take for granted until we start coughing or choking on something. The actual mechanism of how a swallow happens is complicated and I'm not going to drone on about it here. If you're really interested, you can look it up online (lots of Youtube videos detailing the process) [88]. Suffice it to say that it involves a bit of chewing and moving of food around in the mouth, getting it to the back of the mouth to initiate the reflex to swallow, requiring muscles and nerves to control all the movement. The opening to the airpipe closes off (again requiring involuntary nervous impulses to do it properly), down goes the food or fluid into the oesophagus which is the tube that takes it down to the stomach, you momentarily stop breathing when this happens and then the airway opens up again. It is an incredibly complicated but marvellously elegant procedure. However, there is also a lot to go wrong with it.

For numerous reasons such as deterioration of nervous impulses, inability of the brain to sequence how the whole event should happen (for instance after a stroke in which damage has happened to the brain) or weakness of the actual muscles involved in the procedure, the ability to safely swallow can be compromised. Sometimes this is obvious and let's be grateful when it is, at least we know we have a problem. You'd know this when you attempt to swallow something and it 'goes down the wrong way', an event we've all experienced at some time in our lives and not an occasion for concern if a 'one off' event. But when that becomes the usual state of things and you

---

[86] https://www.pulsetoday.co.uk/news/workforce/four-in-10-gps-want-to-leave-the-profession-in-the-next-five-years/ Accessed 6th July 2021, checked 18th December

[87] https://www.rcslt.org/ Accessed 22nd June 2021, checked 18th December 2023

[88] https://www.nidcd.nih.gov/health/dysphagia Accessed 22nd June 2021, checked 18th December 2023

cough after most meals or drinks, then there is a problem which needs to be sorted out and promptly too. The worry is that although you are coughing like a good 'un after food and fluid are going down, that indicates that some of it has gone into an area where it should not trespass. Your body is doing the best to get it out from that area by getting you to cough it up. For all that you may be making an almighty racket doing all of this, you don't know for sure that you have got it all up. With some people the reflex to make you cough has gone and the substance goes into the lungs unannounced. You may have 'silently aspirated' something into your lungs [89]. It is highly unlikely to be sterile given the fact that it was in your mouth in the first place thus you now have an amount of a foodstuff...peas are a classic one, or a bit of biscuit, that provides a fantastic place for microbes to flourish and you develop 'aspiration pneumonia' [90]. Cue feeling very rough indeed, a trip to your nearest District General Hospital and a course of intravenous antibiotics +/- a spell in Intensive Care or a bout of septicaemia and possibly death.

You can of course, avoid this whole drama by requesting assessment by a Speech and Language Therapist at the earliest opportunity. In hospital, if the staff notice you choking or coughing on food and drink then they will request the assessment for you. But if you are at home, phone your GP's surgery and request a community SaLT visit. The SaLT will come and assess your ability to safely swallow from the comfort of your own home and will advise what can be done to make it safer.

This can involve such tactics as thickening fluids (prescribed thickeners from the GP will do that) to almost give the throat and the whole swallowing mechanism something to get to grips with and provide more of a 'mass'. Other actions that might be recommended are mincing food so that there are no lumps to deal with and making food moist as well. Dry and lumpy food is hard to get down at the best of times. They may also suggest things like swallowing every mouthful twice...so swallow once, you think you've got it down but before you put another forkful into your mouth, swallow again. Another trick could be, don't try talking and eating, do one or do the other but not both at the same time (that is a good rule for anyone, not just those of us that have 'incompetent swallows' (the technical term is dysphagia) as a view of the contents of one's dinner partner's mouth is not the nicest dining experience).

Not only do SaLT deal with swallowing problems but they also do what their title implies...speech and language assessment and therapy (and sometimes provide adaptations to deal with problems) [91]. All the many and various nervous activities that are involved in swallowing hold true for speaking though a lot more of these are under voluntary control. Nonetheless, if the muscles of the throat are weak or the nerves not carrying the appropriate signals correctly there is potential for things to go awry. Thus, communication becomes a bit of a problem. Words are not articulated properly; people don't understand what you say...incredibly frustrating. This is not down to your listeners being a bit hard of hearing (well, sometimes it is!!), this is the result of you being unable

---

[89] Roland, J., *What does aspiration mean?*, healthline, updated June 25th 2019, Accessed via https://www.healthline.com/health/aspiration on 22nd June 2021, checked 18th December 2023

[90] https://www.nhs.uk/conditions/pneumonia/ Accessed 22nd June 2021, checked 18th December 2023

[91] https://www.rcslt.org/ Accessed 22nd June 2021, checked 18th December 2023

to articulate properly. If this starts to happen, it's not going to go away of it's own accord, you need to be assessed and given the best professional advice. So don't delay.

Once assessed the SaLT may prescribe a set of exercises to help you strengthen your facial, oral and throat muscles if that is appropriate. Or they may be able to provide you with aids to communication, boards with pre-written out sentences or a computer tablet to help you.

You can access private Speech and Language Therapists, some set up in their own practice. The role of the SaLT also includes a lot of dealing with young children and those with long standing neurological problems, so ensure the one you want to see has expertise in dealing with older adult problems. Like all Associated Health Practitioners, SaLT's need to be accredited by their governing body whether in private or NHS service and this is with the Royal College of Speech and Language Therapists [92].

Occupational Therapist

Occupational Therapists are a trained profession that also require accreditation. Much like doctors or nurses, they have their own professional body whose requirements they must need meet to practice and this is the Royal College of Occupational Therapists [93]. Their role is to help you maintain the ability to do those everyday things that life consists of – boiling a kettle and making a cup or a pot of tea, cooking for yourself (we're not talking haute cuisine here, a very simple snack is sufficient such as beans on toast), ability to wash and keep clean [94]. Often in hospital you will meet an Occupational Therapist who will do their best to get you home with any equipment or alterations to life that will help. Occupational Therapists do not routinely see every single patient in hospital, the nurse looking after you may have some concerns regarding how you will manage when you go home (you saying the usual "I'll be alright" won't cut the mustard here I'm afraid, you actually have to demonstrate you'll be ok. It is in your interest to allow the professionals to consult with you. Of course you are at liberty to take their advice and suggestions or not but the staff looking after you have a duty of care, a moral and legal obligation to ensure they have done the best for you and offered you any extra support or assessment they think you may need). Your children, next of kin, neighbour, anyone who knows you may voice concerns to the staff that you are not really managing that well at home. If such is the case you will be referred to the OT and they will come to see you and talk with you about what they can offer, how they can help. Sometimes, if your recovery from whatever brought you in to the hospital in the first place is slow, they may take you off to the "OT kitchen" and put you through your paces making a cup of tea or a slice of toast. They want to make sure you don't starve when you go home. If getting onto and off the bed is a problem whilst you're in hospital, they will want to ensure that it is possible once you get home. They may well assess you doing that and they will do it with a bed at the same height as

---

[92] https://www.rcslt.org/ Accessed 22nd June 2021, checked 18th December 2023

[93] https://www.rcot.co.uk/about-occupational-therapy/what-is-occupational-therapy Accessed 18th December 2023

[94] https://www.nhs.uk/conditions/occupational-therapy/ Accessed 22nd June 2021, checked 18th December 2023

your 'at home' bed. If they can make suggestions or offer equipment to help, they will. Such things as 'leg lifters' for folk with really heavy and swollen legs are one of the things they can supply. Or maybe little blocks for the bed legs at home to sit in so that your bed is at a better height for you.

If they are at all concerned about how it will be when you get home, they may well take you on a 'home visit' and you, the OT and possibly your carer or next of kin or whoever you request can come as well. They will assess how your house is set up for you to manage at home. They may suggest actions such as taking up the rugs as they are a trip hazard or moving a bed downstairs and using a reception room as a bedroom, putting in a ramp to get to the front door, widening the doors for a wheelchair to have easy access, getting a shower seat or a stair lift. You don't need to feel threatened or aggrieved by any of their suggestions, they are trying to give you the best of their professional opinion and extensive experience, plus they know what little tweaks and pieces of equipment can turn a daily trial into an easy action. Other things they can provide are perching stools to enable you to perch at a high work surface and cut vegetables or tinker with watches or crack safes or whatever particular hobby you have. They can provide rotating car seats to enable you to get into the car with greater ease. Electric can openers or cutlery with large handles to make gripping them easier. Plates with rims so that those with visual problems can eat safe in the knowledge that they are not spilling their grub all over the tablecloth. Non-slip mats for the bath and special keyboards if you need one to make life work for you. They are an absolute treasure trove of knowledge and expertise, they want you to go home and be safe.

If you think you would benefit you can access the vast knowledge of an OT whilst you're at home, phone your GP's surgery and ask to be referred to the Community OT. Of course, the GP's surgery will want to know why, it may be that another professional would be of more use to you. Bear in mind also that **NHS Occupational Therapists are busy**, with a fair load of clients so you may wait a little time for them to assess you. But they will come eventually and if they can offer help they will.

Another way to access them is through the private route and there are lots of Occupational Therapists who practice privately. Ensure that they are registered with their governing professional body (the Royal College of Occupational Therapists) though I am quite sure they will bring that to your attention very early on into any tentative enquiry. The benefit of this method is that you won't need to wait and indeed if you have private health insurance, it may even come as part of that. If you feel you would benefit from the expertise offered by an OT and you can afford it, go for it. You'll get what you need (advice and possibly equipment) quicker. You are of course completely at liberty to accept their advice or reject it but don't allow any reluctance to change scupper your life of ease and make it difficult.

Dentistry

Just because you are an older person does not mean you can let your teeth and mouth hygiene go. If you have even just one of your natural teeth left, you need to clean it (or them) twice a day as you have always done. Really…the whole brushing twice a day routine. Plus, if you have dentures or a plate you need to clean that twice a day as well. You get to choose if you sleep with your dentures or plate but they need to be clean. There are unfortunate results of folk letting their dental and mouth hygiene drift off with the advance of age. Not only can it lead to painful mouth conditions which make eating a problem and then compound any weight loss, it can also lead to systemic problems:- infection around the heart; heart disease and heart attacks; an increase in the rate of cancer; an increase in the probability of developing dementia; respiratory infections and erectile dysfunction [95] [96] [97]. I have nursed people who have developed some of these conditions as a result of poor dental hygiene…so shape up in the teeth department, folks! An emergency trip to hospital and a month long course of intravenous antibiotics would be really embarrassing if it was caused only by your squalid routine (or lack of it) in the tooth department. You are not Albert Steptoe, don't channel his personal hygiene habits!

You've heard it all before I'm sure, there are bits of food left in your mouth after eating, trapped in the grooves between teeth or layering up on top of the gums. They provide a fabulously welcoming environment for bacteria which left to their own devices will multiply and can get into the bloodstream – hence all those systemic problems I mentioned above. They will also cause infection of the gums which of course is painful and can lead to something as dramatic as septicaemia [98] and will also cause teeth (those few remaining ones you have left) to loosen, allowing even more bacteria into the gums. The tooth will eventually fall out or need to be taken out because it's so painful. Mouth ulcers can be caused by this mechanism also (though not just by this, rubbing dentures or food too hot can cause an ulcer as well, as can a dry mouth) [99]. So… the whole sorry scenario can be avoided by decent attention to dental hygiene. Clean your teeth and floss between them…I know when I was a young person that flossing wasn't advocated, I don't even remember floss being for sale but you can't refute the fact that it makes a difference and arguing that you got to your age without using it is a little reductive. If something is scientifically proven to improve our human lot…why would you not do it? I mean colour televisions were not around when you were young, but you happily watch them now (though whether they improve the human lot is questionable!).

Another thing…if you have a complete set of dentures and none of your natural teeth left, you still need to clean your mouth twice a day [100]. A quick brushing of the tongue with a toothbrush (not too vigorous here, you're not out to sanitise it, just clean it) and a good swishing of the mouth with either warm water or a mouthwash is needed. This is to keep the whole glorious arrangement

---

[95] https://www.nhs.uk/live-well/healthy-body/health-risks-of-gum-disease Accessed 24th June 2021, checked 18th December 2023

[96] https://www.oralhealthgroup.com/news/poor-oral-hygiene-can-lead-to-erectile-dysfunction-infertility-1003936757/ Accessed 24th June 2021, checked 18th December 2023

[97] Houston, C., The Link Between Dementia and Dental Health, medcinae.org, 2019-07-08, Accessed from https://www.medicinae.org/link-between-dementia-and-dental-health Accessed 24th June 2021, checked 18th December 2023

[98] https://www.sepsis.org/sepsisand/dental-health/ Accessed 24th June 2021, checked 18th December 2023

[99] https://www.nhs.uk/conditions/mouth-ulcers/ Accessed 24th June 2021, checked 18th December 2023

[100] https://seniorsafetyadvice.com/oral-hygiene-care-for-seniors-with-no-teeth/ Accessed 18th December 2023

happy and in working order so that food tastes as good as it always used to and your appetite does not diminish as a result of poor practice. Don't forget that your lips are part of your mouth too, if they become dry and cracked, life will lose a little of it's savour, keep them in good order and make like a supermodel, brush them twice a week (not for as long as your mouth though, only a quick once over) and when you've finished your routine, anoint your lips with a moisturising film... Vaseline is useful but there are a ton of others in the chemist or on the supermarket shelves. A moisturising gloss can be useful for those of us that want a bit of colour as well.

If you have a dentist, keep going for check-ups and treatment. Don't think that because you're older that you won't get toothache or mouth problems. Dentists do a lot more than look at teeth, their annual inspection is also on the look- out for signs of systemic or local disease so make an effort and go. If you do not have a dentist because you've let it drift.... get back on a dentist's list and go to the check-ups. If mobility is a problem and you really cannot get out of the house your dentist may well be able to come to you. In an emergency you can find a dentist by dialling the 111 service [101].

Deal with any dental pain swiftly. The body sends pain signals to bring it to your attention so that you can do something about it. Get in touch with your dentist, arrange a consultation and get it sorted. If you don't have a dentist then take prompt action and phone for an emergency one. You might take the opportunity whilst you're waiting for an appointment or visit to really assess if you've been doing your mouth cleaning routinely and adequately and upping your game. Also, no dentist wants to be confronted by a dirty mouth that smells (and they can, believe me!) or is coated in gunk.

Whilst waiting for the dentist to deal with the pain, consider using pain killers (technically referred to as analgesia and I'm going to carry on with that term form here onwards). Gentle everyday ones such as Paracetamol or Aspirin can be effective but I leave it to you as to which one you choose. You know best if you are allergic or can't tolerate either of those. You may want to also consider the group of drugs known as Non Steroidal Anti Inflammatories - drugs such as Ibuprofen or Voltarol. Now these drugs are not without side effects [102] and if you've never taken them before be aware that they don't agree with everybody. But if you can take them with no problems, they can be useful in toothache.

If a mouth ulcer is the problem, there are various gels that can be obtained from the chemist to apply directly onto the ulcer to relieve the pain. Make no mistake, this is not healing it, just helping you cope with the pain of it. Good dental hygiene will help it heal (and would have helped it not develop in the first place). It should clear up within a week or two [103]. If it lasts longer than three weeks or is persistent in erupting, gets larger, bleeds or becomes red or painful – see your dentist

---

[101] https://www.nhs.uk/nhs-services/dentists/how-to-find-an-nhs-dentist/ Accessed 18th December 2023

[102] https://www.nhs.uk/conditions/nsaids/ Accessed 26th June 2021, checked 18th December 2023

[103] https://www.nhs.uk/conditions/mouth-ulcers/ Accessed 26th June 2021, checked 18th December 2023

or your GP [104] as dealing with the possible conditions that may be causing it are best sorted out earlier rather than later.

Physiotherapy

The role of the Physiotherapist is vastly under rated outside of hospitals or GP surgeries because most people only come into contact with them when something is amiss. Although you can access their service when you are out in the community is usually along the line of pulled and sprained muscles or particular aches and pains that will lead to your meeting. But the Physiotherapist's role consists of so much more. Consider…they are able to help you recover from illness or injury and they are also able to help you avoid it in the first place. Another fabulous professional who can help you make life a bit better, a bit easier and altogether much more enjoyable. They are able to give advice, prescribe movement and exercises to help with specific problems and recovery from events or conditions such as heart attacks or a stroke, a hip replacement or disc surgery, whiplash injury or osteoporosis. They can help with relief of pain by movement of body parts and to encourage easier movement and therefore less pain in the future [105] [106]. Some of them even offer acupuncture or hydrotherapy in private practice.

NHS physiotherapy services can be accessed through your GP, sometimes all you need to do is fill in a form and 'self refer'. This is the sort of thing that will help if you have something like a frozen shoulder, hip pain whilst you're waiting for a hip replacement or are wondering how to cope with living with Chronic Obstructive Pulmonary Disease (Physios are experts at helping out with chest complaints). If you go into hospital, either as a planned admission or as an emergency and the doctors and nurses feel you would benefit from physiotherapy they will ask for you to be seen and that will be a routine occurrence for any hip or knee or any joint replacement. Sometimes, depending on local protocol, the Physio may be the folk that get you out of bed first (though don't be surprised or alarmed if it is the nursing staff that help you to get out of bed initially) after a joint replacement. If you've had a stroke you will be routinely referred to physiotherapy as they can help with avoiding mobility problems later on. Same with a heart attack, the aim of the game is to get you up and moving as safely as possible as quickly as possible, so you may well see a specialist Cardiac Rehab Physio. All these people are here to help you regain as much mobility and independence as possible. They will suggest activities and possibly equipment that they believe is professionally indicated. You are of course at liberty to discount their advice or suggestions at any time…but they are the experts.

You can of course, access the services of a Physiotherapist privately and this will cut out any long wait. As with Occupational Therapists they will need to prove their registration with a governing

---

[104] https://www.nhs.uk/conditions/mouth-ulcers/ Accessed 26th June 2021, checked 18th December 2023

[105] https://www.csp.org.uk/careers-jobs/what-physiotherapy Accessed 26th June 2021, checked 18th December 2023

[106] https://www.bupa.co.uk/health-information/muscles-bones-joints/physiotherapy Accessed 26th June 2021, checked 18th December 2023

body to ensure they are able to practise [107]. If you search online you'll find local ones to you and you can give them a quick phone call to roughly discuss whether they can help you and lead on from there. Simple things such as prescribing a set of arm exercise to strengthen the upper limbs can lead to more functionality and thus a better quality of life. Leg and balance exercises will help prevent (but never totally eliminate the risk of) a fall. The advice and treatment of a Physio is a useful resource in the quest to maintain the life you want.

The whole point of physiotherapy is to help you as the whole person, lead the life you want to be able to lead and to continue leading it for as long as possible. It is a degree-based profession, taking three years to qualify and incurring a student debt to gain that degree. There aren't a surfeit of Physiotherapists.

Dietician

The role of the dietician in keeping body and soul together cannot be underestimated as one gets into later life [108]. Often, appetite decreases with advancing years…we allow ourselves to become less mobile and so we don't build up an appetite. We mistakenly believe that we need to eat a lot less forgetting of course that the body needs a certain amount of fuel just to keep all its many and varied functions adequately working [109]. Whilst you may not need to eat the same amount that you did at twenty years old when you were digging ditches for a living…you do still need some food. I often see elder folk with immense lassitude who eat next to nothing and it is difficult to know if the one is a result of the other. Also, the ability to taste and savour may have declined [110] or it may have become physically more difficult to prepare adequate food [111], thus the amount ingested is less than it needs to be.

A good rule of thumb is to be aware of any unintentional weight loss. You don't need to rush out and buy a set of bathroom scales, but be aware of the looseness of clothes, appraise yourself in the mirror. If shirt collars are becoming looser it is unlikely to be down to a sudden deterioration of the quality of the cloth and much more likely to be you losing weight. If skirts are now hanging off you that were previously a little snug – well, it's not good to lose weight without paying attention. We, as a society, are continually reminded of what a nation of obese folk we are and yet… malnutrition in the elderly is a huge and worrying problem. If you think you've lost weight and you

---

[107] The Chartered Society of Physiotherapy is the main professional body, their web site is https://www.csp.org.uk but not all physiotherapists will be registered with them. The important registration that enables them to practice is with the Health and Care Professions Council https://www.hcpc-uk.org/ Accessed 18th December 2023

[108] https://www.bda.uk.com/about-dietetics/what-do-dietitians-do.html Accessed 18th December 2023

[109] https://dieticiandaily.com/2017/12/14/diet-in-old-age/ Accessed 26th June 2021, checked 18th December 2023

[110] https://dieticiandaily.com/2017/12/14/diet-in-old-age/ Accessed 26th June 2021, checked 18th December 2023

[111] https://www.nhs.uk/conditions/malnutrition/causes/ Accessed 26th June 2021, checked 18th December 2023

have done this unintentionally then ask for a dietician assessment. Dieticians have all sorts of clever ways of assessing body mass without you actually getting onto a set of scales.

They are the professionals who study for three years at degree level to gain an understanding of how the body works in relation to food and are the experts at working out exactly how much in the way of food and intake you need to keep yourself well and properly nourished. The usual route of accessing their services if at home is to phone the GP surgery and ask for an assessment (this is becoming a bit of a regular thing isn't it? Me telling you to phone the GP's surgery but hopefully you'll get an understanding of why they are quite so busy every time you want to phone them. The GP surgery acts as a hub or contact point for all these marvellous services) although of course you can access a dietician privately (note however that only a trained Dietician is allowed to called themselves such; a Nutritionist, whilst they may be helpful, will not have had the same training [112]).

I cannot stress enough quite how debilitating it is to become malnourished and underweight. You may think it is nothing more than a little bit of lassitude and slenderness, unfortunately the health implications are far more serious than the need to go down a dress size and to rest a little more as you're so tired.

As you age, your body slowly loses muscle mass, even if you're fit, well, healthy and active. We can notice this with anyone of advancing years, the muscles underneath the skin in various areas of our body has lessened (hence wrinkles in the face and slack skin on the back of the hands). But if you're not any of those four things, if you're unwell, malnourished, have low levels of moving about then the process accelerates and becomes a bit of a downward spiral. And it ultimately means that you have a much higher chance of becoming frail, ill, disabled or dead. Whilst you can't prevent the decrease of muscle mass that age brings, you can do your best to delay it or to ensure the loss is a little as possible.

Why all the fuss about losing muscle mass? Well, it is the amount of muscle you have on your body that helps you stop losing your balance, it enables you to walk properly, lifting feet up off the ground and not shuffling. Maintain an erect posture and not 'furniture walk'. As you lose muscle mass, you become less and less able to do such things as climb the stairs, go out for a walk, get off the sofa - and the less you are moving about, the faster the muscle loss happens [113] [114].

There is a huge amount of research going on into this condition (called sarcopenia) and it seems to be related to hormones changing as we age and the way protein is synthesised and used in the body. And it turns out that elder folk need a lot more protein than previously believed as one of the reasons that the muscle decreases in amount is due to the muscle cells getting smaller in

---

[112] https://www.bda.uk.com/about-dietetics/what-is-dietitian.html Accessed 18th December 2023

[113] https://www.health.harvard.edu/staying-healthy/preserve-your-muscle-mass Accessed 3rd July 2021, checked 18th December 2023

[114] https://www.healthline.com/nutrition/sarcopenia#TOC_TITLE_HDR_6 Accessed 3rd July 2021, checked 18th December 2023

response to the amount of protein in the body [115] and the body's ability to produce and use proteins. The upshot appears to be:- eat more protein (eggs, meat, fish, nuts and nut butters, lentils, dairy foods); take up resistance training as no matter how old you are when you start, there is some benefit. If you haven't done any exercise for a long time, don't go at it like a bull in a china shop, take advice from your doctor before you go hell for leather on this. Ask for a referral to the gym. You may be able to have a service called 'Gym on Prescription' (this differs from area to area but no harm in asking). Take the advice of a gym instructor that is used to or trained in working with elders.

Podiatry/ chiropody

Another professional that may be of great use is a podiatrist/ chiropodist as they can help with foot care. The difficulty in taking care of feet becomes more obvious as we age if we lose suppleness and the ability to get to the right level to cut our toenails and clean our feet thoroughly. Some medical conditions (diabetes, peripheral neuropathy, rheumatoid arthritis, peripheral vascular disease amongst others) carry with them a susceptibility for the feet to suffer and cause further problems. Also, as part of the natural aging process, skin becomes drier and the pads underneath your feet become thinner which can lead to difficulties in mobilising, general aches and pains can cause a reluctance to move about and feet can become mildly deformed with bunions or claw toes [116]. All this doesn't need to impact too greatly on your life and your health if you access the services and advice of a podiatrist who will treat your feet and help with future care instructions for you.

If you do have difficulty getting to your feet and giving them good care, then access a private chiropodist/ podiatrist. Like most things I talk about in this book, it will only deteriorate unless you do something about it. If you have carers to help you wash or bathe then ask them to pay attention to your feet if you feel they're skipping that area (although it is recognised as an important area in maintaining hygiene amongst care staff). If obtaining shoes that fit and don't hurt are a problem do not be tempted to shuffle round in slippers, this causes you to do exactly that...shuffle, plus they are not a good support and make you more liable to fall. The Royal College of Podiatry recommend running shoes if you find yourself in that situation [117].

Podiatrists need to have completed a three year degree and gained qualification as such, plus they need to be registered with the Health and Care Professions Council [118]. You can access a registered

---

[115] De Pietro, "Sarcopenia: What you need to know", July 21st 2017, https://www.medicalnewstoday.com/articles/318501 Accessed 3rd July 2021, checked 18th December 2023

[116] http://cop.org.uk/common-foot-problems/ageing-feet Accessed 5th July 2021, checked 18th December 2023

[117] http://cop.org.uk/common-foot-problems/ageing-feet Accessed 5th July 2021, https://www.bda.uk.com/about-dietetics/what-is-dietitian.html

[118] http://cop.org.uk/become-a-podiatrist/what-is-a-podiatrist Accessed 5th July 2021, https://www.bda.uk.com/about-dietetics/what-is-dietitian.html

podiatrist by searching on the website of the Royal College of Podiatry [119]. If getting to their surgery is difficult , you may well find one who does home visits.

Social Worker

Nowadays the role of the Social Worker is vastly different from that understood by the generation of our parents and grandparents. For a start, this is a degree profession with stringent supervisory requirements for its' members [120]. Moreover, the information that Social Workers need to know to do their job effectively is vast, I mean huge. They need to understand legislation, guidelines, proposed best practice, ratified best practice, the latest research in their field of expertise, any change in any legislation that relates to their field. They need to know how to tell people unpalatable information. They need to be able to keep the welfare of their client as paramount to their working aim as their remit is to help the client achieve the best life they can do so within the constraints of that person's life and situation [121] [122]. They need to know the resources available for their clients not only locally but nationally and they need to be really good at interdepartmental and inter-professional liaison.

Social workers once trained, tend to specialise in particular areas of expertise so the one that may be involved with you or your family will have experience in the field of 'older adult' social work. It's not a particularly well-paid job and it has a huge amount of stress involved in it. They need to re-register every two years and need to complete further training to do so. Each devolved country has it's own regulator for Social Workers. Mostly, Social Workers will work either for the Health Authority or for the Local Authority but occasionally you can find one in private practice.

The reason they need to know all those details about you and how much in the way of assets you have, who is your next of kin, what sort of house you live in and other stuff that may seem really intrusive is that they need to get a really good idea of your ability and resources so they can get the best available for you. These are the people who will endeavour to set up a package of care should you need one, be on the lookout for a residential home place for you if that is appropriate, deal with other agencies should that be called for. If you have a Social Worker that is involved in your care then this is the person to contact if you have any queries or complaints about your carers or if you feel you are vulnerable or being abused by anyone (family members included). Theirs appears to be a thankless task, if anything ever goes wrong, it's always the Social Workers that cop it in the newspapers...but how much we need their expertise. For every patient that is in hospital and cannot go home safely, they will find carers or a placement for them to go to. They will be

---

[119] http://cop.org.uk/ Accessed 5th July 2021, https://www.bda.uk.com/about-dietetics/what-is-dietitian.html

[120] https://new.basw.co.uk/ Accessed 18th December 2023

[121] https://www.communitycare.co.uk/2010/09/20/what-is-the-role-of-social-workers/ Accessed 6th July 2021, checked 18th December 2023

[122] http://www.indeed.com/career-advice/career-development/what-is-a-social-worker Accessed 5th July 2021, checked 18th December 2023

involved in meetings with the patient and the next of kin, the staff of the ward, the medical team perhaps so they are a vital part of the team effort to get you home and happy.

If you're at home and feel that you need help (or perhaps such has been recommended by the Physiotherapist or the Occupational Therapist) then you will need to phone or get in touch electronically with your Local Authority and arrange for a Social Worker to come and visit you and assess what help you need, and advise you on any help you can have or are entitled to claim.

Conclusion

A large and diverse array of professions have been presented here. Who knew there were so many folks dedicated to keeping you well and coping ably at home. If you need their assistance, get in touch with them, if they can't help, they may well know someone else or some other profession who can.

Useful websites and resources

https://www.bbc.co.uk. Needs no introduction I think. A useful resource for news though of course not without a slant.

https://www.bda.uk.com/ The website of the British Dietetic Association, a professional body and a trade union, they give information on a slew of subjects including a section especially for the older adult. They are not a regulating body.

https://www.bupa.co.uk/ A private healthcare provider, they give details on their services. Yes of course, they're touting for your custom, but they do provide good information.

https://www.communitycare.co.uk/ This site is devoted to helping Social workers stay up to date with the latest legislation and recommendations and acts as a job hub and a resource of relevant articles.

http://cop.org.uk/ The Royal College of Podiatry website, it has a 'find a podiatrist' function and a section for patients that gives basic information regarding a number of foot problems.

https://www.csp.org.uk The Chartered Society of Physiotherapists, it has a search function enabling you to check or find a physiotherapist and a useful section on dealing with common complaints that would warrant physio input such as backpain or COPD.

https://dieticiandaily.com/ This is a blog so the information provided does not always come with overtly noted scientific or research based back up. However, as a resource or a pointer to go forward with a subject that interests, it is useful.

https://www.gponline.com   Providing daily news and articles aimed at and of interest to GP's.

https://gprecruitment.hee.nhs.uk   The website of the administrative part of the GP training programmes. As there are nationwide educational criteria to be met before anyone can qualify as a GP, the NHS oversees the whole process and provides timelines for those who want to apply.

https://www.hcpc-uk.org/   The website of the Health and Care Professions, there is a function enabling you to check that the professional with whom you wish to deal, is in fact on their register. This is the body that provides the educational programmes for training of the professions and who set the standards to be met for registrants.

https://www.health.harvard.edu/. The website of the Harvard Health Publishing group which is part of the Medical School of that University. Priding itself on being 'the most prestigious and trusted source of medical education in the world', it thus publishes stuff that is evidence based and up to the minute. Their newsletters are published quarterly and they also provide digital courses, special health reports of subjects that may be of interest to readers of this book. All of these require payment of course.

https://www.healthline.com/. The website of Healthline News, it reports on 'emerging research' and purports to have everything checked by a 'panel of experts'. Certainly, their articles are written by one person and a named other person has checked the facts. The site has a slightly more political slant than the following site but as it's all about informing ourselves, all to the good.

healthcareers.nhs.uk   An NHS website that deals with various careers available in the NHS (of which there are a surprisingly huge number) and goes into details of what is involved in both the career and the training for such.

https://www.medicalnewstoday.com/   An American health information site, they promote a 'science-led, facts-first' approach, they note 'strict sourcing guidelines' and aim to provide the information to enable all of us to live our healthiest lives based on the latest research.

https://www.medicinae.org/   'Student run and peer reviewed', this website and journal publishes articles that slant towards the history of medicine...or so it says. Quite how '4 Ways to Take your Fitness to the Next Level' meets that criteria is beyond me. However, there are articles that deal with dental health, nutrition, exercise and fitness.

https://www.nhs.uk   The website for the NHS with lots of information, how to find services you might need, check up on drugs you are taking, conditions you may have, there is also a video library dealing with more common conditions and advice on healthy living.

https://www.nidcd.nih.gov/   An American government website, the 'National Institute on Deafness and Other Communication Disorders' aimed at practitioners involved in the fields of hearing, speech and olfactory senses. It has an extensive site index and provides a heap of information. Note though that as it is an offshore site, advice re legislation and help available may differ from what is actually available in the UK.

https://www.oralhealthgroup.com/   I believe this may be a Canadian website, the online presence of a published periodical for dentists. It contains news and articles.

https://www.pulsetoday.co.uk   is a publication for UK GP's

https://www.rcot.co.uk/about-rcot   The website of the Royal College of Occupational Therapists, they have a large section on finding an occupational therapist, useful questions to ask and they provide a range of leaflets detailing how an OT can help.

https://www.rcslt.org/   This is the website for the Royal College of Speech and Language Therapists, their professional body, they give professional guidance to their members and promote research and quality. It does not regulate Speech and Language Therapists though.

https://seniorsafetyadvice.com/about-us-2/   Another American site, run by two professionals who have an interest in older adult care. Extensive and useful information on a variety of subjects, from safety in the home to dealing with older drivers. Well worth a visit.

https://www.sepsis.org/about/our-mission/   A USA site with an interest in sepsis, a charitable organisation. Interesting information with a useful acronym to remember.

CHAPTER 5

Hospital and hospital visits

Thirty-five years of nursing and many, many (forty and counting) hospitals informs this chapter so I haven't used references. I advise that which I have long thought could make life easier for patients. Therefore, feel free to totally ignore what I say here...but I would really recommend the ear plugs even if you don't want to take any notice of the rest of it.

Going into hospital as an emergency admission and as a routine

With a long-standing disease process or condition it is likely we will at some time have an 'exacerbation' of the condition, an acute flare up. At these times, hospital treatment may become necessary. So, it is a useful trick to keep a bag packed 'just in case'. Having been a nurse I am going to give you a few suggestions about what would and would not be useful.

Don't bring towels, they are bulky, take up a lot of room in your bag and are not necessary. Hospital staff don't like to use them because the potentiality of them getting lost is huge. Hospital towels (which are washed at a hot wash to within an inch of their lives...so not sterile but pretty darn clean) are used once and then put into the skip for washing. Your towel can't be put into the laundry skip so will have to hang around the ward area, wet and warm and a perfect breeding place for all sorts of microorganisms. Of course, if you are going into a private hospital as a routine appointment you are free to do what you want (but wouldn't you want to get your money's worth by using their towels?). If your towel from home does get used and inadvertently chucked into the dirty washing skip...that's the last you'll see of that. So leave them at home.

You don't really need to bring a flannel either. The same rules apply; where are they going to be hung to dry? Hospitals have their own disposable version of flannels that they will happily supply you with so you can leave them at home too.

Don't bring expensive jewellery or watches with you. Hospitals are not secure places, people wander in and out all day: visitors, staff, contractors, volunteers, doctors, nurses, porters, technicians. The average ward (pre COVID 19 obviously) could have up to 90 people a day passing though that ward (and I worked that out on a small ward) a day. It is not a secure environment. Whilst I would love to say that all will be well, things do get stolen. If you come into hospital as an emergency and you happen to have a lot of money on you then you will be asked if you take responsibility for it. And if you do then it stays with you but at your risk. Otherwise, it can be sent to the hospital safe and will be sent back to you when you are discharged from the hospital. So... don't bring your tiara, your Omega watch or the family silver.

You may need a little cash to buy papers and items off the trolley if one comes around to the wards. Their existence is not a given, they are usually staffed by volunteers. Major city hospitals usually have a barrage of shopping opportunities in the foyer and possibly even a coffee shop for when you're well enough to get down there. May I just add here that hospital staff are not there to fetch and carry for you, they will not go down to the shops to get you a paper unless they have the time. And if they have the time today, they may not have it tomorrow, don't assume they can. But still, a little cash may come in handy.

Hearing aids and spectacles…if you use them bring them, have cases or pots in which to put them and ensure they've got your name on. Things get lost and with the best will in the world, the staff do not have time to see what you're up to and where you are putting your belongings. Don't leave them on the meal tray! The same goes for dentures, bring your denture pot and your preferred method of cleaning them. Label the pot with your name.

Toiletries, all the usual stuff that you use, soap, razor, toothpaste, toothbrush, mouthwash, face cream, make up…bring them. The hospital can supply the bare necessities if you come in without but they are basic.

Tissues, it's not the NHS' job to provide you with Kleenex, bring your own please.

Clothes. It is not obligatory to get into your pyjamas and/ or nightie the minute you are admitted to a hospital. Patients are encouraged to get up and dressed in their clothes as they would normally, it actually speeds recovery time! By all means bring your night attire but that will be for night-time only. You will be expected to get dressed in the day. Obviously, don't bring your designer dresses or your Saville Row suit with you, ordinary everyday clothes are quite sufficient.

Something to keep you occupied:- pens, papers, books to read (but you won't be getting through 'War and Peace' whilst you're in hospital, it is just too noisy and too busy, something short and lightweight is better), ear plugs (it is horrendously noisy….really), notelets to pen missives to friends, puzzle books, magazines, tablet/ computer (but see the above proviso re security), phone (ditto), charger for both, an eye mask to keep the light out at night.

If you like to listen to the radio or a source of music or entertainment at night, bring headphones or ear buds so that you don't disturb other people. You may like to bring a small cheap radio with you if you do because the hospital radio may well not be available in the wee small hours or the console behind the bed may not be working, plus of course there may not be earphones available.

A list of all the medication you are taking, both the stuff that is prescribed by your GP and any supplements that you take on your own initiative. You probably won't need to bring the medication with you unless it is a very weird and wonderful drug or one that you know only you are receiving in the whole of the county. If you want to carry on taking supplements whilst you're in hospital you will need to bring them with you (and you will need to get them inspected by the pharmacist whilst you're in there as they will in all likelihood need to be prescribed by the doctor) as most hospitals do not give supplements. Many supplements are perfectly safe and commonly taken but sometimes some of them may need to be omitted for a day or so whilst you're having other forms of treatment.

Have a list or a piece of paper, or you may even have a pre prepared booklet (some local authorities give them out for citizens (regardless of age) to fill out in advance) on which you have details such as your next of kin or significant other, who you would like to be informed that you are in hospital if you are not in a position to do so yourself. What religion you are, whether you have any dietary requirements such as being vegan or gluten free, beverage of choice, that sort of thing. Also, whilst we're here, are you aware of the 'Message in a Bottle' scheme funded by the Lions charity? This enables you to put relevant details that would be useful in an emergency in a specific bottle and this bottle lives in the fridge. It's not as big as the booklet provided by local authorities but it contains vital information. So if you are found unconscious at home or so unwell you can't organise yourself to give instructions, the ambulance crew will look in the fridge to see if you have one and if so, they'll bring it with you to hospital to enable staff to have vital information without delay.

If you have your emergency bag packed and safely stored somewhere that anyone can find it in an emergency or urgent situation, that will help to make life easy for everyone, yourself included.

A bit more to say here...if you've been struggling at home and think you need carers, get it organised whilst you're at home. It isn't the hospital staff's job to organise your care, though that is mostly what happens. Of far greater use to you is to get your carers sorted when you need them rather than waiting for some emergency to bring you into hospital and hopefully get it sorted then. Remember I said in a previous chapter that carers are not sitting around waiting for you to phone them? They are busy folk and there aren't enough of them to cope with demand. Therefore, if you decide you need carers to help at home whilst you're in hospital, you will be waiting in hospital for that care package to be sorted out. And that could take weeks. Or months. As far as social services are concerned, you are in a place of safety, it is not an emergency to get your care package sorted out. It will happen but who knows when. If you get it organised whilst you're at home, it'll get done quicker.

Having said that...if you do have a care package in existence and you have to come into hospital, that care package will cease to be after a certain amount of time (I believe the rules vary depending on where you live). Well, that is unfortunate but can't be helped.

If the nurses need to refer you to social services they will also need your permission to do so. This has implications for families who want to get the input of social services to help out with their aged aunt but who don't want to tell her. If she has capacity, she must be told and she must give consent for it to happen. If she has capacity, she gets to decide what happens to her.

And please...don't lie about conditions at home, don't say you're managing fine when you aren't. Sometimes of course it is quite obvious that you're not managing, but if you're doing an effective impression of coping, staff may not be aware. Don't tell the staff that your daughter will care for you when she won't (because she has a full time job, three children and lives 40 miles away). Don't try and fudge things. That is the whole point of this book really. Face up to the truth and deal with what is rather than what you would like it to be. That way everyone who is able, can help you deal with any problems and prevent any further ones developing we hope.

People you will see in hospital

Your Consultant...is the chief doctor in charge of the team of doctors looking after you. They will have trained long and hard and undergone stringent examinations to get to that position. What they don't know about their subject of expertise is probably not worth knowing. You may not see the consultant every day, but you will see them at least once in your hospital stay. More likely is that you see the other and more junior members of the team...bearing in mind of course that even a newly trained doctor has taken between four to seven years to get to that position, so even the most junior is not exactly a slouch in the brains department.

Your Doctors...are the members of the medical team and you will probably build up a bit of a relationship with them. They are humans just like you, with good and bad days and a fairly stressful job so whilst they'd probably love to stop and chat, they have another twenty patients to see before they have lunch (if they get any!). Be kind and help them as much as you can by being clear and informative if you have anything to say and formulate questions in advance so that you get the answer you require.

The Nurses...you may have a team of nurses that are 'your' team or you may just have whichever nurse is available. Some of those may well be agency nurses who have never met you before. They will do their best to look after you, dish out your medication, ensure you're not in pain and have eaten and drunk that day. They are the generalists who will liaise with other professionals if they think there is a need. They are not clairvoyant, if you have a problem (pain, need the toilet, are constipated, worried about your cat at home, feel really unwell) tell them and they will do their best to sort it out.

The Health Care Support Workers are also the folks you will see more of and they may have time to chat. They will provide 'hands on' care and report back to the nurses if they think ought is amiss or they are concerned or worried about you. They may well be doing technical tasks as well such as taking blood or noting observations. You will build up quite a rapport with these two groups of people and they may well make your time in hospital more fun that you anticipated. But maybe not.

Other patients...on the ward are not there to entertain you or to be browbeaten into your opinion or desired behaviour. If the majority of them do not want the television to be on...you're outvoted I'm afraid. Though having said that some hospitals have an over bed arrangement with personal TV attached (but you'll pay for the privilege of using it). Please bear in mind that the whole point of a hospital is to treat you and get you better. It is not a five star hotel. Or even a four star. Hmmm...to be honest I wouldn't give it three stars as a hotel. But as a place to sort out your acute ill health, it's the business.

It is noisy. The amount of people who have dementia are increasing and these patients do not necessarily have much idea of the time of day, where they are or even what is appropriate social behaviour. Thus you may be on a ward with someone who shrieks the entire night (remember I did advocate ear plugs) or calls for their daughter or gets up in the night and urinates on the floor. Life in hospital can be…interesting! And an education.

The night staff will be needing to look after folk who may be a lot less able than you so will need to switch the light on when they do so as they will be needing to inspect skin colour and any wounds (hence the need for an eye mask in hospital). The phone will still ring at night and the various bits of equipment that are necessary will add their bleeps and whistles to the whole cacophony. Quiet it aint!

Bits of equipment…first off you may come across an automatic observation machine (sometimes referred to as a Dynamap, a bit like a vacuum cleaner in this country is referred to as a Hoover). This will enable the operator to automatically take your blood pressure, pulse, oxygen saturation of your capillary blood and possibly temperature as well from one piece of equipment. Unfortunately it is fairly noisy, and if you don't meet it's arbitrary criteria on what is 'normal' it will bleep. Some of them can be turned down in volume. Most of them can't. It is a beast but that's the way it is. Strictly speaking it isn't necessary if the ward has a manual sphygmomanometer (blood pressure measuring apparatus) but most wards don't and most folk no longer know how to take a blood pressure manually.

If you or the patients near you are having any sort of infusion of fluids and/or drugs then you will come across an infusion pump. Again it's noisy, some of them alarm when there's 15 mins of the infusion left and then again they all alarm at the end of the infusion. If there is some form of obstruction, it will alarm, if the plug is left out of the wall and it's running on battery, it will alarm, if you look at it in the wrong tone of voice it will alarm, no sorry, I made the last one up, but that is what it feels like. Any excuse and the machinery will make a noise.

If you or one of your fellow patients is hooked up to a cardiac monitor (which does what it says on the tin, it monitors your heart…it's not actually doing anything to it), then that may well beep along with the heartbeat. Not so reassuring if you're trying to get to sleep and a bit like a dripping tap. Why ,oh why don't manufacturers make these machines with lights to alert staff and not noises? It doesn't help patients sleep, and a good night of sleep is implicated in a good recovery.

Some patients may have a night time breathing adjunct that clamps across their face and forces a bit of air into the lungs, these make an understandable whooshing noise though one can get used it as it is at least regular.

You may be surprised to find that you can sleep with all this racket going on and for anyone that did their National Service when younger, it may not seem like too much at all. For the more delicate souls amongst us…it can be difficult to get used to. Do your best. If you feel you need sleeping tablets to help you get to sleep, mention it to the nurses and they will request the doctors to prescribe such, Be aware that there may be good medical reasons why prescribing you a sleeping tablet is not a good idea, they are not withholding it willy nilly.

Visiting Patients in Hospital

Consider first who benefits from visiting. We hope it's the patient and to that end please don't come in an enormous crowd, there isn't the room for you. Hospital wards are not vast empty spaces, they're crammed with equipment, beds, trolleys, bedside cabinets, tables, chairs for the patients, trolleys full of paperwork. There really isn't room for eight of you to gather round the bed. Moreover, being ill is actually an exhausting business. If the patient can summon the energy to deal with you, that comes at the expense of energy needed to recover, recuperate and regain strength. One or two visitors are quite sufficient to let folk know they're not forgotten.

Keep the noise down. People when ill get very noise sensitive and as I have already said, hospitals are noisy places. Keep topics of conversation general and not contentious, we don't need spikes in blood pressure please. Be aware that the running of the hospital and the treatment of the patient will still continue so it is possible that you will come to visit someone and they will be off the ward having an investigation or being put through their paces by the physiotherapist.

Be prepared to be asked to take dirty clothes away for washing. As I said earlier, patients are encouraged to get up, get dressed and sit out during the day if they are able. But as hospitals cannot launder patient's clothes, it stands to reason that they get soiled or grubby with time. Therefore bring some fresh ones if you are able and be prepared to take dirty ones away with you. If the patient has soiled their own clothes, they will be given to you in a special bag that may be placed directly into the washing machine. Check this first though. I'm not intending to give you false information but if a ward has run out of the special bags at a particular time then any bag will do.

Bring little things to eat or drink that don't conflict with the persons dietary needs. So if you know they have diabetes, don't bring them cake or boiled sweets. Fruit would be more appropriate (but not too much, most folk lose their appetite a bit and I've seen whole fruit baskets thrown away mouldy before now). Your visit is not to supplement their diet but to remind them that you are thinking of and care for them, a few little somethings are appropriate, great carrier bags heaped with stuff are not.

Suggestions for presents to take to people in hospital

4711 Eau de Cologne wet wipes or just plain ordinary wet wipes

A box of tissues

A small fake flower arrangement (alas the days of real flowers in hospital have long since gone and what a loss they are) but only if they're going to be in for a long time. Not worth it if they're going home in a day or so. They do gladden the heart though of patients, visitors and staff though.

Magazines and/or newspapers.

Hand cream.

Lip balm...but be aware that petroleum based lip balm is very much frowned upon now if not downright forbidden. Look around for non petroleum based.

Fluffy bed socks if they suffer from cold feet (but be aware they will need to be loose and non constricting).

A new nightie or pair of pyjamas.

A shawl or a wrap.

A small jigsaw puzzle.

Toiletries.

A book of puzzles and a pen.

An eye mask to help with sleeping at night.

Ear plugs to help as well.

Colouring books and colouring pencils...there are adult colouring books available and they are surprisingly therapeutic and calming.

Whatever creature comforts you know they would appreciate, linen napkins, their own pillow and pillowcase, a rug to go over the bed, their own mug.

Photos of family and friends

Art done by the grandchildren.

If you know they are having trouble eating enough (and you've spoken to the staff to corroborate this) then consider bringing one or two pre-packed puddings. Things like a one portion trifle or a small carton of fruit fool. Bear in mind that any foodstuffs will need to be labelled with the patient's name and kept in the ward kitchen fridge and may well be forgotten there, especially if the patient doesn't remember to ask. Alert the staff to offer at or between mealtimes or you could give it to the patient when you arrive and eat your own with them (it is off putting to be the only one eating, eating with other people is far more socially acceptable and will help get extra calories in).

A get-well card...really, this is not Christmas or birthdays, you don't need to bring a gift. You, a card and a bit of a chat may be just the thing. The gift of you making the effort and turning up to brighten an otherwise boring day is enough.

But whilst we're on the subject of cards let me suggest something that may be really helpful. Most patients get cards and they kick around on the top of the locker for a day or so before they're scooped into a manageable heap and left there. Most hospitals do not have the space for festoons of cards to be tacked to walls (very much frowned upon anyway, can't use Blu-Tak or Sellotape for infection control reasons) and there probably isn't anywhere to hang a string of them. Buy a scrapbook and take it with you, and some Sellotape and help or leave for the patient to put the cards in the book. They'll then be able to look through them whenever they fancy, can add to them as cards arrive and they won't get in anyone's way.

If you can't visit because you're miles away or for some other reason, consider the morale boosting effect of letters fairly frequently written. Or a postcard a day with a cheery message. That can really brighten someone's day.

Presents for hospital staff

You do not need to give any staff a gift and in fact you may not give a particular member of staff a particular gift at all. Or more to the point, they may not accept it, their professional registration forbids it. So if you do want to give something as a token of thanks, give it to the whole team.

Let me also talk about cash donations to the 'ward fund' or 'for the staff'. Don't do it. It goes into a specific account (a 'charitable' fund) that is controlled by a particular department to which the ward sister or manager will have to apply for permission to spend it. It will not be allowed to be used for the benefit of the nurses at all, it will only be allowed to be used for patient's benefit and only for equipment that the NHS doesn't supply routinely. So things such as a blood pressure monitor will not be allowed to be bought, as that is equipment that the NHS should supply. Items such as sofas or chairs will be allowed and unfortunately televisions as well (I know, I know I'm possibly the only person in the country who believes that televisions should have no place in a hospital and that it should be quiet and restful). If the money accrues in the account (and they do because the conditions for spending that kindly donated money are rare and stringent), the money will be sequestered and used for other things (such as buying televisions on another ward that doesn't have such a large fund). I say this because I have direct experience of this. All over the country there are accounts running into hundreds of thousands of pounds that no-one can spend. So please…don't give money to the ward.

If you want to give money to a specific ward project (say a garden for the patients to enjoy) then that is a different thing. It is the general "for the nurses" or "for the ward" that isn't useful.

If you want to give the staff something to show you are grateful for the care you received here is a list of possibilities:

Coffee, tea, decaffeinated versions of both, herbal tea bags, cold brew water flavourings (the staff have to provide their own coffee and tea!)

Pens (likewise the staff have to provide their own), black ink biros are best

A basket of fruit (in fact a couple of bags of apples, oranges, bananas and pears from the local supermarket would be more than welcome).

Cartons of fruit juice.

If it's warm, ice lollies (though bear in mind that they may be nowhere to store them so a cool bag borrowed for the occasion might be useful).

Small tubes of hand cream or a dispenser of hand cream (big pots aren't useful due to cross contamination issues), fairly bland as staff are not supposed to wear or use highly perfumed products.

If you're going to buy sweets or cakes or biscuits for the staff, please consider that gluten free options may be welcome. Crisps are a useful substitute and welcome due to the novelty.

I will reiterate here that you do not need to give anything to the staff, they are paid to give you your care, you have contributed towards the cost of it throughout your working life. They do not expect it, they are always pleasantly surprised when it does happen. Having said that, the 'thank you' cards are usually kept somewhere so people can look through them and if you have received care over and above that which you expected, please mention the person you wish to thank by name. They can then use that in their re-registration documentation.

So hopefully that's given you the heads up about what to take into hospital. Let's hope you don't have to go in…but if you do….take ear plugs (oh….did I say that earlier?)!

CHAPTER 6

On living as well as you can

This is going to be a general chapter around living as well as you can without mentioning any specific symptoms. If you are living with a chronic disease state or in less than optimal health then it is pointless wishing you'd done things differently in the past. We are where we are and we're all wise with hindsight. No, the thing that is going to improve your quality of life as you move forward is to keep on top of the symptoms and prevent it getting any worse or to slow down progression as much as possible. Living with a chronic disease is not a bundle of laughs, but neither is it an excuse to give up and wallow in misery. Life still has good moments and occasions regardless of any physical state we're in. After all, it is our thinking and our reaction to the external events that make us happy.

Check ups and keeping up to speed with your health

Firstly, the medical folks that are in charge of your health (the Consultant or the GP) will want to have regular checks on your condition. This could be anything from weekly or monthly to annually. It very much depends on the state of your health and if you have any other conditions going on at the same time. Keep up with and go to the check-ups in good time. Just because you're scared of what the medics might say is not a good reason to not turn up. If you haven't been sticking to the party line and behaving how you should best behave to be of good health, then just shape up, go, listen to a bit of a lightweight ticking off and suck it up. Not turning up for the appointment is a hugely rude way to behave, you are wasting the time of those specialist folk who are there to help you, you are wasting the time of the ancillary staff who are also there to help you (transport technicians, the clerk who keeps the outpatient's clinic running as smoothly as possible, even the very folk who empty the bins in that consulting room in which you are seen…all of these people are here to make life better and easier for you) and you are potentially depriving someone who actually and urgently needs to see that consultant or health professional and couldn't because there wasn't enough space on the list that day. Plus you are costing the NHS a fair bit of money [123]. If you're going to squinny out of turning up, at least have the good grace to cancel your appointment a few days in advance. And if you do that, if you cancel a few days in advance (and kudos to you if you do alert the outpatients department…you may have just saved somebody's life by allowing them to be seen early enough in their disease to make a difference) then remake the appointment whilst you're on the phone. Given enough DNA's (Did Not Attend), you will be erased from that consultant's list of patients and you'll be back to managing it on your own (or not as the case may be!). Now, there is no reason why you shouldn't have the best treatment as should

---

[123] https://www.gov.uk/government/publications/reducing-missed-hospital-appointments-using-text-messages/a-zero-cost-way-to-reduce-missed-hospital-appointments Accessed 2nd April 2022, checked 27th December 2023

everyone else but part of that is showing up for the regular checks. Don't grumble that things aren't going well if you can be bothered to show up for the MOT's and service!

May I also mention here that it is in your best interest to research and find out about any disease process you are undergoing as much as you can ...if you have internet access (you're on Yahoo, Google, Facebook, Instagram, X previously known as Twitter, TikTok, any other social media platform then you're on the internet and you have access) you have the ability to look into this in great and enabling depth. So don't use the fact that you are going to have to do some mental work around this to let you ignore it. You've been given a brain, now is the perfect time to put it to some use.

Researching around health and the best treatment available and what new and groundbreaking stuff is also happening needs to be approached like a campaign of war. It is of no use to just throw yourself in and hope for the best, you need to draw up a plan. If you have the ability, the time and the interest, you could then start looking at scientific and medical research around this subject. What is happening out there in the big wide world of science? What are the latest findings and developments that are up and coming? Again, a word of caution. Be aware of where this information is coming from, a 'paper' from a high street supplier of dietary supplements may not carry as much scientific validity as a researched experiment that occurred in a university and has been peer reviewed and published in a reputable scientific magazine. Of course, it may carry that much validity, that is why you need to exercise caution and judgement and use your time on the interweb wisely. It is very easy to get sucked down a rabbit hole (I'm sure you've experienced that at some point) but remember...all the time you're on social media endlessly scrolling through videos of cats and dogs, cake icing and balloons and so on...you're making someone some money. Not you though, you are giving your time and your life away to someone you haven't even met. So, draw up a plan of research around your particular condition of interest and go for it systematically so that you are in the best position to know about your health.

Medication

Second piece of general advice for living with a long term and/ or chronic disease or not so grand health. Take your tablets and medicines! Patients not taking their medicines is costing the NHS about £300 million every year [124]. Take the medication that you have been supplied at the time recommended by the consultant or the GP, so if they advise take it in the morning two hours before breakfast then set your alarm and do it. If it needs to be taken in the evening before you go to bed, then do that. Pharmacologists and doctors spend years training to be able to wisely and accurately tell you what medication you need to take and at what time. Yes, it can make a difference to the efficacy of the drug. Be aware of any 'precautions', again they're noted for a reason, if it says avoid grapefruit then do so.

---

[124] http://www.medicinewaste.com/http://www.medicinewaste.com/ Accessed 27th December 2023

Take your tablets. And yes, you may have to take a large amount per day depending on your condition. I lose count of the number of patients I have met that moan about the amount of tablets they need to take. Really? Moaning about the fact that pharmaceutical science has provided you with drugs that work and keep you ticking on? If you find them too onerous to take just consider how life was before all this stuff was invented. What happened to people with your condition twenty-five years ago? Fifty? A hundred years ago? Right, enough said. If taking a heap of tablets is physically difficult because swallowing them is problematic then space them out a bit. Some before, some during, some after breakfast. Likewise any lunch or evening ones. If swallowing really is problematic then ask your doctor or pharmacist if you can have that medicine in a different format, as a liquid, as dissolvable, as a patch, as a suppository. Make life easy for yourself by working out how to do this in an elegant way that does not involve harping on about the tedium of taking tablets. And take them! I cannot stress this forcefully enough. If your consultant has prescribed you a drug it is because they think it is the appropriate one for you and your condition. Don't just not take it when you get home. If you don't want to have that particular drug then tell your consultant before she writes the prescription for you, save the NHS some money. Because I do hope you realise that once a box of tablets goes out of the chemist and into your home, it can never be used for anyone else, even if you've never even opened the box. So if you don't want the pills, don't accept the prescription. You are a partner in the care of your health along with the GP or the consultant and her team…talk to them about your meds, explain why you don't want a particular one or why you do want a different one. Reach a compromise or even a stalemate, but don't just take the box and then not take the contents.

Sometimes folk have a bona fide reaction to a particular medication. Some people are downright allergic to stuff (various antibiotics are the usual culprit but there are others too) and if you are allergic to a drug then you will have an allergic reaction to it. An allergy is a different thing from an intolerance. An allergy will provoke the signs and symptoms of a reaction from your body that this medication is proving too hot to handle. Symptoms such as a runny nose, itchy eyes, a rash, puffy lips or eyes, feeling faint (I mean really, not just an attack of the vapours!), a wheeze, itchy weals on the body [125]…all of these are a result of an allergic reaction, your body going into overdrive dealing with something it's not happy about. It usually happens within a few minutes to a few hours of taking or being exposed to a provoking substance [126] If you take a new drug and it provokes any of the symptoms or signs of an allergy stop taking it and alert the doctor or consultant as soon as you can. I will just emphasis here that if you have an allergic reaction to any drug (or to anything really, bee or wasp stings, egg mayo sandwiches, mussels, there are a heap of things that could trigger this) and you have difficulty breathing or your tongue, lips or throat start to puff up, you feel confused or you collapse or feel like you are going to do so go to your local A and E pronto as they can give you something to calm the whole situation down.

---

[125] https://www.nhs.uk/conditions/allergies/symptoms/ Accessed 3rd April 2022, checked 27th December 2023

[126] Dorfman, Ruslan, 'Drug allergy and drug intolerance: What is the difference?' accessed via https://www.pillcheck.ca/2019/06/06/what-is-the-difference-between-a-drug-allergy-and-drug-intolerance/ on 3rd April 2022, checked 27th December 2023

Back to tablets and new medication then. If you get symptoms like a runny nose, a bit of belly ache, a bit of aching in the limbs, a bit of fatigue, and it takes a few hours to a few days to come on, well that is not an allergy, that is intolerance. And whilst you still want to stop taking the medication because it clearly isn't right for you, it is not a situation that requires a trip to casualty. Again, let you GP or your team know asap, so they can have a rethink about which medication to try next or replace the disagreeable one with. And if you are ever asked if you're allergic to any drug you can say "Not allergic but I am intolerant of…". And of course, your doctor doesn't know you're allergic or intolerant of it if you've never had it before. All medication has to undergo stringent testing before it's allowed out into the field (with the exception it seems of vaccinations provided to deal with new diseases in times of national panic) of being prescribed for the general public so whatever it is, it won't have provoked too much in the way of allergies whilst it was being trialled. Sometimes, if a particular drug belongs to a 'family' of similar drugs then it is assumed that you are allergic to the whole lot (Penicillin is a good example to use here…if you're allergic to Penicillin, then reasonably it is a given that you cannot be prescribed any members of that 'family'; Flucolaxacillin, Amoxycillin, Ampicillin and loads of others that will end in '…cillin' you see the family 'surname' here to alert you that it's part of the same group). So if your new medication provokes a reaction in you, don't hold the GP or consultant to blame, they're doing their best, just alert them so they can note it down for all future consultations.

So take your medication, take it at the time it is prescribed to be taken, observe any warnings that come with it (such as 'avoid broad beans and marmite'). It is as simple as that. Every box of tablets or medicine that you are given will contain a leaflet (a 'data sheet') on which is written a huge amount of information about that medication. It will tell you the conditions for which it is prescribed, it will tell you of various doses that may be prescribed, it will give a list of potential side effects (a word about side effects here…side effects of drugs do happen. Sometimes it is the side effect that is the reason the medics have prescribed the drug (a classic case of this is a variety of anti- depressants whose side effects proved to be making people sleep well…so now they're prescribed as sleeping medication primarily) but it is not a given that you will get any side effects at all. They need to be fairly rare for the licence of the medication to be given in the first place. So by all means read the 'data sheet' but don't get too alarmed by what 'could' happen, I mean, we 'could' all get run over by a bus tomorrow but we don't stop going out and about because of that potential). It will give advice about any particular conditions that need to be met before you take the medication (on an empty stomach or on a full stomach or do not take with indigestion medication, that sort of thing), it will tell you what to do if you miss a dose or take too much of a dose. Interesting reading and as you are chucking these tablets down on a daily basis, it behoves you to keep up to date with what you're doing. Knowledge is power, ensure you know what you are taking and why.

Actively being as well as you can be

Third piece of advice is to keep your physical body in as good a shape as you can. Stop smoking and /or vaping. Smoking is known to cause ill health and various conditions and for all the publicity around it…vaping is no safer. Look…when I was sixteen and took up smoking (yes well, we are all young and foolish at some point no?), popular belief was that smoking less than ten fags a day was perfectly fine and not injurious to health. We now know it is hugely damaging to health but it took time for that to filter through from scientific circles to common knowledge. We are in roughly the same position with vaping now. You're still inhaling nicotine which is a dangerous drug with side effects [127]. Taking nicotine as gum or as a patch has the same malign effect, the drug is still going in there, by skin or mucous membranes, it's all the same to your body. There are charities that can help you conquer your nicotine addiction and the NHS also will help. Get in contact with your local surgery, they will have information. Or try www.nhs.uk/smokefree or there are helplines such as Quitline…the help is out there, but ultimately, you are the one that has to do this.

Food and maintaining weight

What and how much you eat becomes important in older life as taste and the ability to smell can decrease, causing appetite to pall. Difficulties in agility and mobility can also lead to taking the easy route of packet soup in a cup and nothing but carbohydrates (the stodgy stuff) for the rest of the day. If shopping or cooking become difficult then the path of least resistance is to default to an unhealthy 'snacky' diet and forget about cooking a decent meal. Whilst you may be sat around at home, nowhere near as mobile as you were in your 20's, you do still need to eat enough for your body to work effectively. It takes energy for the physical body to just continue on, just to exist (this is referred to as your basal metabolic rate – the amount of energy needed just to keep body and soul together and the body ticking over with enough energy to meet it's needs [128]) and that energy comes from food. Regardless of whatever eating plan you favour (vegetarian, vegan, pescatarian, gluten free, Paleo, Clean, reducing) it is a fact that you need the grub to keep going. And the better the fuel you give your body, the better the results for you. Regardless of how you stand theologically, you can believe that God gave you this body and this life or that you are a complete accident of a random universe made of stardust- regardless, it is a miracle that you're here and you have a body as a vehicle to be here. Give it the respect it deserves and treat it with care, attention, and compassion. And eating soup in a cup and marmite on toast on a daily basis is not due care and attention. Try to get as varied a diet as possible. Ring the changes with vegetables. If preparing from fresh and raw is difficult use frozen or tinned, they very often have as much nutritional value

---

[127] https://www.drugs.com/sfx/nicotine-side-effects.html# for a comprehensive list of side effects. Accessed 27th December 2023

[128] https://www.sciencedirect.com/topics/neuroscience/basal-metabolic-rate Accessed 3rd April 2022, checked 27th December 2023

as fresh [129]. Ensure you get enough protein in your meal [130]. If you are able to eat fish then attempt to have some during the week, it provides good nutrition and is associated with prevention of some of the ailments that may come with elder years [131]. Tinned is better than nothing and is easily sorted out with less mess. If you are able to take dairy foods, go onto full fat unless advised otherwise by your consultant or dietician. Desserts though palatable are to be thought of as an added extra. Sugar doesn't count as a food, more of an addictive poison. So if you do have dessert make it a good excuse to have fresh fruit (though it can be cooked of course). Sugar gives your body nothing except calories, no vitamins, no protein, no fats. Same with alcohol. Unintentional weight loss needs to be avoided; I have spoken about this earlier in Chapter 4 so I won't labour the point here. Note that I say 'unintentional'. Deliberate loss of body fat because one is obese is another kettle of fish but one that must needs be taken equally as seriously. Of course, as any person who has ever been 'on a diet' (have there ever been more depressing words in any language?) knows, the minute you are told not to eat something, it becomes the very thing you want to eat. Now this is not a 'diet' book, my main concern here is to alert people to the health difficulties that come if you stop bothering to eat properly. If you need to lose weight, reduce, slim down for health reasons, there are a million and one ways to do it. You can ask for help from your GP, there are diet companies aplenty (but don't you find that a little suspicious?...I mean if diets worked we'd only ever need to do it once in a lifetime wouldn't we?), there are books enough to fill a library on how to trim down. You are the captain of your ship, you are responsible for yourself, do the research, evaluate what is being said, ask yourself the question every time "Who stands to make money or gain from this?". And go at it slowly.

However, if getting enough food in is the problem then consider introducing healthy snacks into the day. I am not talking about a packet of crisps and a candy bar here. I mean food stuffs that will give you some beneficial nutrients. An apple (can't eat a raw one? Eat a bowl of cooked apple with a splash of double cream), a chunk of cheese, a spoonful of a nut butter, a cup of cocoa made with whole milk, a boiled egg dipped in salt and pepper or mayonnaise, a cold cooked sausage left over from last night, a full fat yogurt, a small bowl of dhal, a small bowl of cooked, cold broccoli with grated cheese on top, any of the above will give you a little extra, one or two of these a day as well as meals will help halt the speed of weight loss.

Whilst we're on this subject, I have noticed a lot of folk tend to drink less as they get older. AgeUK recommend a fluid intake of between 1.2 litres and 1.6 litres [132] which is just under three pints. The body needs an adequate fluid intake just to keep all the cells and organs working, keep the

---

[129] Brown, Jessica, '*Frozen, fresh or canned food: What's more nutritious?*' 28th April 2020 accessed via https://www.bbc.com/future/article/20200427-frozen-fresh-or-canned-food-whats-more-nutritious on 3rd April 2022, checked 27th December 2023

[130] Morais, J.A., Chevalier, S. and Gougeon, R., "*Protein turnover and requirements in the healthy and frail elderly*", J Nutr Health Aging, Jul-Aug 2006; 10 (4): 272-83 Accessed via https://pubmed.ncbi.nlm.nih.gov/16886097/ on 4th April 2022, checked 27th December 2023

[131] https://www.webmd.com/diet/health-benefits-fish Accessed 4th April 2022, checked 27th December 2023

[132] https://www.ageuk.org.uk/salford/about-us/improving-nutrition-and-hydration/drinking-well
Accessed 29th March 2022, checked 27th December 2023

blood flowing without becoming thick and sludgy, keep the eyes working and the mouth moist. So, do not allow yourself to become dehydrated. Keep a glass or bottle of water near you and if you can't bear the taste of it, add a little squash or make it into a herbal tea. Get the fluid down because you do need it.

Sex and the older participant

Long considered to be a pastime of the young and to fade into insignificance as one ages, turns out elder folks like sex just as much. After all, kids have left home, work may have finished, the house is up to scratch, pension coming in, garden sorted, that leaves plenty of time to devote to the erotic arts.

It will be no surprise to you I'm sure but bodies change as we get older as does sexual response, due to a number of factors; body image, difficulty in arousal and pain on intercourse being some of the culprits in women [133] and for men erectile problems, a lower sexual desire and difficulties or changes in ejaculation [134]. Not in everyone, some folk keep their lusty appetites through advancing years, in others the spirit is willing but the flesh is weak. What to do? Because it is an enjoyable part of life and brings one closer to one's partner. Well, firstly if you have any disease processes going on (diabetes and cardiovascular disease are the common but not the only culprits here) that may well be impacting on your sexual response, speak to your GP or your Practice Nurse. There may be a medication they can tweak a bit that may prove helpful, they may be able to refer you to a specialist in that area. Hormone levels tail off a bit as we get older, get those checked. I'm not suggesting that your medical provider will automatically give you HRT or testosterone to get you back to pre middle age levels but it is worth checking to see if anything can be done. They would also be wise to check for depression as well which can be another reason why desire goes out the window. Again, I am not suggesting that anti-depressants are the correct answer here, everyone is different but there are other ways to deal with mild depression [135] it behoves you to do the research around this area.

Anyway intimacy doesn't need to be sexual for a start, Sunday mornings in bed with a cup of tea and being physically close can provide intimacy, laughing uproariously at a joke only the two of you know about can be intimate, flirting with your spouse of fifty years can be intimate. It's all in the intent and appreciation. The physical act of sex is not necessary for intimacy and it not even associated with it for some folk. So, if intimacy is what you're after and your sex life has gone south, explore other ways to spend time with your significant other that bring the two of you together in closeness and *bon accord*.

---

[133] https://www.nia.nih.gov/health/sexuality/sexuality-and-intimacy-older-adults Accessed 27th December 2023

[134] Chung, Eric, 'Sexuality in Ageing Male: Review of Pathophysiology and Treatment Strategies for Various Male Sexual Dysfunctions', Med Sci (Basel). 2019 Oct; 7 (10): 98, accessed on 2nd April 2022 via https://pubmed.ncbi.nlm.nih.gov/31547182/ checked 27th December 2023

[135] '*Treating depression without using prescribed medication: Booklet for patients and carers*' Scottish Intercollegiate Guidelines Network, 2010 accessed on 2nd April 2022 via https://www.sign.ac.uk checked 27th December 2023

Female post-menopausal genitalia (really is there no nicer word? It sounds so clinical… but then euphemisms sound prissy) undergoes changes some of which can be dealt with. Aridity of secretions that used to smooth the way to a thumping good shag now causes soreness for both parties. There is a topically administered form of HRT which can help with this, inserted into the appropriate area twice a week, it relieves the dryness [136]. You could always try lubricants, there are many available (Yes, Sylk, Replens, Durex) specially made to replace the moistness and ease things. They come in oil based and water based varieties, with or without applicators and they don't contain any active drugs so if the HRT isn't appropriate for you, these will help. Make it part of the intimate time or prep beforehand, it's up to you.

Erectile dysfunction does increase with age though this may be due to the other diseases that we get as we become older. Anything that interferes with blood flow or nerve impulses to the penis is going to have a detrimental effect, so that includes cardiovascular disease, diabetes and any neurodegenerative illnesses [137]. So whilst you may not be able to be rid of the disease process, take the best care you can of yourself with it to lessen the effects. There are pharmacological treatments but these are not suitable for everyone [138] there are also surgical treatments or adjunctive equipment (well, you know, any port in a storm!). Testosterone replacement therapy does have a place in this conundrum but not for everybody as it is Hormone Replacement Therapy and does carry with it risks to health if not properly titrated.

Joint replacements or wounds can interfere with positioning and so you'll need to experiment. Total hip replacements necessitate being careful with the angle into which you put your hip, throwing legs into the air with glee is not quite as easy so care must needs be taken. Gently does it, we don't want dislocated hips or knees. If you go into hospital for a joint replacement, ask the surgical team for advice on sex following the operation. It'll do them good to realise that sex doesn't stop at whatever age they are plus fifteen years. They will be able to tell you about any restrictions on positioning.

Breathlessness and breathing difficulties can also play a part in restricting what you do, frenetic activity of yesteryear may no longer be possible but a gentler approach may result in the same 'feel good factor'. Gentle experimentation may be called for here, I'm all for taking it easy but if this is an important part of your life then it is well to try and find ways and means of expressing your affection and getting your jollies. Alteration in body image can also change things. If you have lost a limb or have a chronic wound, it may be difficult to merge that image with the younger one you had of yourself. And indeed, no point trying to go back to the past. But you can use it as a new way of being and one that expresses sexuality still…because it's important to you. We're not all supermodels or body builders. By the time we get to our age we've realised that beauty and attraction comes in many guises and form. Hopefully your partner looks as gorgeous to you now

---

[136] Obviously speak to your GP or Practice Nurse about this as it is a drug and not suitable for everyone.

[137] Chung, Eric, 'Sexuality in Ageing Male: Review of Pathophysiology and Treatment Strategies for Various Male Sexual Dysfunctions', Med Sci (Basel). 2019 Oct; 7 (10): 98, accessed on 2nd April 2022 via https://pubmed.ncbi.nlm.nih.gov/31547182/ checked 27th December 2023

[138] Watch 'Something's Gotta Give' with Jack Nicholson and Diane Keaton for an amusing take on this matter.

as they always did (only with the addition of some interesting wrinkles and maybe a few extra stone to grapple with). Age brings wisdom (and wrinkles) so let's not let our perceptions of 'what we've lost' ruin it for us. Let's celebrate the fact that we're still here, lines, curvy bits and changed anatomy and all, sexual expression is not a private preserve of the young of the species…even if they do think they invented it!

Keeping Active

Keep active, keep mobile, it will have benefits not only for your mobility levels but for balance and thence less liability to falls and hopefully better sleep as you put your muscles, joints and ligaments through their paces.

Start from where you are, it's no use rueing the fact that you're not as active/ mobile/supple as you previously were when younger. Start from here and start from now. If you need a bit of inspiration look at these articles [139] [140] [141] and whilst I am not suggesting that we can all become marathon runners or competition winning body builders, any increase in activity, mobility and suppleness is a boon. The benefits of remaining or gaining an active life are many including a stronger immune system, a healthier heart, it reduces the risk of falling [142], it decreases cognitive decline [143], enhances bone health, reducing the risk of type 2 diabetes, stroke and cancer [144]. Another benefit of increasing activity is that it can be made to also increase social engagement. You could become part of a group that does a regular exercise.

AgeUK have a section that deals with increasing one's activity [145] and also provide links to activity videos to do at home. If you're able to get out and join a local gym or walking group or go swimming in the local pool or take up Zumba classes then go for it. Take advice from your doctor or the practice nurse if your health is not as good as it could be. Don't go hell for leather on this one and if you can find a trainer (and even the local health and fitness centre should have one) to help you steadily gain mobility and strength all the better. But when it comes right down to it, any activity is better than none. Any movement is better than slumping on the sofa.

---

[139] https://www.weareageist.com/profile/julia-linn-65-best-life-now/ Accessed 1st April 2022, checked 27th December 2023

[140] https://www.weareageist.com/profile/joan-macdonald-74-journey-to-strength-and-fitness/ Accessed 1st April 2022, checked 27th December 2023

[141] https://ernestineshepherd.net Accessed 1st April 2022, checked 27th December 2023

[142] https://foundation-therapy.com/here-are-3-benefits-and-reasons-of-staying-active-as-you-age Accessed 1st April 2022, checked 27th December 2023

[143] https://heritagesenior.com/blog/2022/02/15/staying-active-in-aging Accessed 1st April 2022, checked 27th December 2023

[144] https://www.nhs.uk/live-well/exercise/exercise-health-benefits/ Accessed1st April 2022, checked 27th December 2023

[145] https://www.ageuk.org.uk/information-advice/health-wellbeing/exercise/exercises-for-older-adults/ Accessed 1st April 2022, checked 27th December 2023

If your current mobility is such that even standing up is a bit of a problem then there are still ways to increase your activity levels, the NHS website offers exercises online [146] alternatively there are adjuncts available online such as pedal exercisers or a mini stepper that will allow your legs and feet to get some action. Small and lighter weight weights can also be bought online to help with upper body strength and consider resistance bands that are also effective, have a look at the exercises offered by livestrong.com [147]. The trick is to start slow and with the lightest weight and only build up once you are comfortable (well, not too comfortable, it's supposed to be a little bit of a push but then again, not something that lays you out with fatigue and muscle aches for days afterwards). Consider also whether an online seated yoga class might be a session you'd enjoy. You'd certainly benefit from it. There is a wealth of information, advice and classes available online and locally, you need only to do a bit of a search and you'll find something.

Pain

Chronic pain is mostly caused by inflammation but there are times when pain killers (analgesia) are the correct and right way to deal with pain. I am not talking about acute pain here. Acute pain is a sign that something is dramatically wrong NOW, with your body. A broken leg will cause acute pain, treading on a nail whilst barefoot will cause acute pain, hammering your thumb by accident will cause acute pain. All of these examples show you that your body is trying to tell you something is wrong and to do something about it now.

Chronic pain isn't quite like that, for some reason what was acute pain has stayed in the system and gone on for longer than it should have done. It's no longer serving the purpose of telling you to do something about it now! Things to try to see if they help. You could alter your diet as I have mentioned previously and see if that helps at all. You could try other lifestyle tweaks to see if they help. NHS Scotland have a good web site explaining chronic pain and drug free ways of dealing with it [148] such as mild exercise, doing enjoyable things, relaxing. But if chronic pain won't go or hasn't yet, then pain killers are a good choice and they come in differing sorts. I'm not going to discuss here the stronger pain killers that will need to be prescribed by a doctor, they are a step up the 'pain ladder' . What I'm dealing with here is 'homely' medicines to counter pain.

A hot water bottle or a cold pack is a good place to start, certainly research has shown it works with acute pain [149]. With both of those, hot and cold, make sure there is a layer of something

---

[146] https://www.nhs.uk/live-well/exercise/strength-and-flexibility-exercises/sitting-exercises Accessed 2nd April 2022, checked 27th December 2023

[147] https://www.livestrong.com/article/13730101-quick-full-body-seated-dumbbell-workout/ Accessed 2nd April 2022, checked 27th December 2023

[148] https://www.nhsinform.scot/illnesses-and-conditions/brain-nerves-and-spinal-cord/chronic-pain Accessed 2nd April 2022, checked 27th December 2023

[149] Dehghan, Morteza and Farahbod, Farinaz, 'The Efficacy of Thermotherapy and Cryotherapy on Pain Relief in Patients with Acute Low Back Pain, A Clinical Trial Study' J Clin Diagn es. 2014 Sep;8 (9): LC01-LC04 abstract available on https://www.semanticscholar.org/paper/The-efficacy-of-thermotherapy-and-cryotherapy-on-in-Dehghan-Farahbod/74bd59b70b85a7ff6b776c61191d83869e75de2c accessed 27th December 2023

between you and the hot or cold. Most hot water bottles come with fluffy or knitted covers but you also need something between you and the cold pack. A hand or bath towel folded around it should do well…it has the capacity to damage the initial layer of skin, just like a hot water bottle if there is no protection. Keep an eye on the skin surface of the area you're treating and give yourself a regular break from it so you don't end up with burns or frostbite. We've all seen the legs of our grandparents who consistently sat too near the electric fire, that is what you want to avoid. So whilst warmth or cold on an area of pain is a relief, be careful that it doesn't cause damage. Those of you that have diabetes or any sort of neurological disease or condition, would not be best served by this treatment. Damage could occur without you feeling it, so go without and move on to my next suggestion.

The homely paracetamol is a fabulously good pain killer if you weigh more than 50 kg, don't take more than 8 tablets in 24 hours and stagger the dose so that it is two tablets every six hours so as to give you an even effect of the analgesia. Beware of cough mixtures or 'compound' pain killers that contain paracetamol, so don't take more that 4 grams or paracetamol in 24 hours in total. For those of you that weigh less than 50 kg (which is 7 stone 12lbs) just take one paracetamol tablet every four hours and don't take more than 4 tablets a day [150].

Asprin is an analgesia that doesn't suit everybody but if you can take it, up to two 300mg tablets every four to six hours will help but this is not to be a long term thing as asprin does have side effects that can be worsened in the elderly. If you do want to take it long term then you must only have one 300mg tablet every four to six hours [151].

Other pain killers that can be bought over the counter are a group of drugs called Non Steroidal Anti Inflammatories (NSAID's) (such as Ibuprofen and Diclofenac) can be considered though can be irritating to the stomach lining (if it gives you indigestion or belly ache stop taking it, do not mask this with anti-indigestion medication, that belly ache is there to warn you that the drug is not agreeing with you. Take heed and stop taking it). Best taken on a full stomach and if you really can't countenance something to eat, at least have it with a glass of milk or a spoonful of peanut butter. Again there are limits regarding how much you may take in 24 hours and it does interact or potentiate some drugs so have a care and do your research first. Pay attention to the instructions on the box.

There are creams and ointments that can be applied to the skin on areas where there is pain. These can contain the Non Steroidal Anti Inflammatories that I mentioned above. They are obtainable over the counter but if you need more than a basic dose, the doctor will need to prescribe them. There are also creams or applications that contain what might be considered 'alternative' or have no active ingredients at all such as cooling strips to put on the forehead in the event of a migraine or arnica cream or homeopathic medicines. These can work very well and for all they may be 'alternative' I would recommend trying them because, you never know, they may do the trick for you. Read the instructions with all of these treatments as they will tell you of the

---

[150] https://www.nhs.uk/medicines/paracetamol-for-adults/ Accessed 27th December 2023

[151] https://www.nhs.uk/medicines/aspirin-for-pain-relief/ Accessed 27th December 2023

'contra indications', the reasons why you shouldn't have this treatment or if you need to take less for any reason.

As well as taking pain killers, think about what time you get maximum effect from them. Taking them before bed time can promote a good night's sleep without being kept awake by pain. If you know that being active in the morning causes pain then taking them in the morning with breakfast makes sense. Another thing to know is that these pain killers, all at the lower end of the pain killing spectrum work fabulously well if taken regularly and at spaced out intervals during the day. You need a certain amount of the drug in your body to do the work. If you leave it too long between doses then your body needs to build up to having that amount in your blood again - taking a double dose is not advocated and can be dangerous. Take the medicine regularly and in the correct amount until the cause of the pain is gone. But don't 'sit' on the pain either. If it is chronic and proving a problem then get to the GP or discuss with the Practice Nurse how your pain could be better managed at home. Never be tempted to take more than the prescribed dose, it could be dangerous (yes, really, I have seen the results of patients doing just that...not good!)

Wherever you live in the UK, your local NHS Trust or Health Board will have a Consultant and/or Specialist Nurse who deals solely with pain, it may be that referral to them may eventually be warranted. Be aware that this is not the immediate path of treatment when it becomes obvious that your pain is chronic, there are lots of other things that can be posited such as relaxation, Cognitive Behavioural Therapy and teaching on biofeedback. These may well be suggested by the Pain Team. Chronic pain in joints can sometimes be treated with injections of analgesia or steroids and though some GP's do this at their surgery, it is more likely to happen in a hospital setting, certainly if the pain is in your back/ spine.

Conclusion

Now look, I could've gone on about loads of things here but I kept it to a few subjects that I thought might be important. But with all of these subjects above the main information seems to be...take charge of your own health, arm yourself with the knowledge and seek help or advice earlier rather than later, keep eating, keep moving, keep enjoying yourself as best you are able!

Useful websites and resources

https://www.ageuk.org.uk is the UK's leading charity dealing with aging, they provide a myriad of useful things, a helpline (0800 678 1602, available every day from 8am until 7pm), huge amounts of information on a massive amount of subjects that are roughly grouped together as 'Money & legal; Health & wellbeing; Care & support; Work & learning', they run a telephone befriending service and a 'real life' befriending service, can put you in touch with your local group who may well know of a local handyperson, they run day centres, provide personal alarm services and stairlift information and sell incontinence products.

https://www.bbc.com As well as doing news, sport and weather, the BBC offer articles on a varied amount of subjects

https://www.bnf.nice.org.uk The British National Formulary and the publications under that title are the *sine qua non* of drug information for the UK. All the drugs that can be prescribed are detailed in the publications and online, including side effects, indications, contra indications, cost of medication, interactions, details on how often it should be administered and how it is presented. Updated twice a year, the paper publications are to be shortly dispensed with and it'll be all online.

https://www.ecigarette.co.uk a commercial website that has shops in south Wales and the Hereford area, they have a range of interviews with various folk that make interesting reading.

https://ernestineshepherd.net is the web site of Ernestine Shepherd an 85-year-old woman who took her health seriously from the age of 56. In incredible shape and health, she now works as a fitness instructor.

https://foundation-therapy.com is an American therapy centre based in Atlanta for better health expressed through physiotherapy, occupational therapy and medical focused yoga.

https://www.gov.uk is a treasure trove of information though it isn't particularly attractively presented. Nonetheless, a good trawl through this website can turn up all sorts of interesting things.

https://heritagesenior.com is a USA community senior living group.

https://www.livestrong.com is an online group that publishes the latest thinking around 'living well, managing weight, getting fit and eating better' with a mission to help people make informed decisions around their health.

https://www.nhs.uk The website for the NHS with lots of information, how to find services you might need, check up on drugs you are taking, conditions you may have, there is also a video library dealing with more common conditions and advice on healthy living.

https://www.nhsinform.scot is a Scottish online directory of NHS advice and treatments and services available. Extensive amount of articles on a large range of subjects and also services provided by GP's, dentists and pharmacies in Scotland.

https://www.pillcheck.ca is a DNA testing site that tailors medication specifically to the patient. It is a Canadian site and obviously out to sell their services but has little snippets regarding effectiveness of various medications.

https://pubmed.ncbi.nlm.nih.gov is a free resource which aims to provide abstracts of scientific articles (mostly to do with the health sciences and related disciplines). They don't automatically include the whole article though if published by themselves they do.

https://www.sciencedirect.com is a little like the above web site but dealing with a huge range of scientific research and aims to 'help you build a solid knowledge foundation' based on the latest research available.

https://www.sign.ac.uk is another Scottish initiative aiming to" improve the quality of health care" and streamline what is offered and available in Scotland. It gives recommendations for practice based on the latest research.

https://www.weareageist.com is a media company which dedicates itself to an online magazine published every two weeks. It aims to offer 'a new vital, vivid cohort who are living life with goals and ambitions not imagined even a generation ago'. They publish an online magazine for free.

https://www.webmd.com is an American site providing reference material for anyone wanting to know more about health. It not only gives up to date information but has blog posts written by folk who actually have the condition they're writing about.

CHAPTER 7

On Dying

This may not be a popular chapter and yet it needs to be thought about. We do ourselves no favours in refusing to contemplate, discuss or plan our exit from this world because we all eventually die. We hope (most of us) for a quiet, easeful death in our bed, at home, either during our sleep or surrounded by our loved ones, whilst lucid, pain-free and in a blissful haze of contentment. This is not always achievable for a number of reasons some of which I'll detail here, along with what alternatives there are.

Some of us will have foreknowledge that death is on the way, we may have a 'terminal diagnosis' ie a diagnosis of the termination or the end of life. This is usually but not always the result of an advanced cancer though I have to tell you now that cancer is not the major cause of death in the UK. Some folk will get the nod from the grim reaper as a result of cardiovascular disease which claims a high proportion of us annually, 11.4 % of all UK deaths are from dementia [152] and the associated problems of that condition. Other leading causes of death in the UK are influenza (not Covid 19), pneumonia and chronic lower respiratory diseases.

A few of us then are going to be be able to plan for this. Given that we've got to go at some time anyway, isn't a bit of advanced warning to be thankful for? Those of us with cancer, cardiovascular disease and COPD may well be able to think about all this and plan in advance. And isn't that a boon? Isn't it rather better to know this is coming? Of course, you're frightened and concerned with the change of condition. Death has a bad rap so none of us look forward to it. We enjoy being alive so the thought that it's going to end and possibly soon, brings a bit of apprehension with it. I believe most of the fear around death is of the physical changes and symptoms it may bring and the thought of what is going to happen to those left behind (in other words an awareness of lack of agency going forward in other people's lives) [153]. So in this chapter I will talk around the physical worries of dying and a little bit about the existential part of it. But first, let's talk about where this will happen.

Where

As a society we are not used to people dying at home and are a little scared of the whole idea. Before the NHS came into being, dying at home was the normal way of things. If you were wealthy enough to call the doctor in and hire a nurse, all to the good. Otherwise, folk just got nursed at

---

[152] Death registration summary statistics, England and Wales: 2022 accessed via https://www.ons.gov.uk/ on 2nd December 2023

[153] Lewis R., *Facts to Calm Your Fear of Death and Dying*, Nov 22nd 2018, accessed via https://www.psychologytoday.com on 2nd December 2023

home by whoever was there. Whole generations were used to the idea of death, dying, the process and how to manage it. We have lost this routine knowledge but if you have the support of the local GP and the District Nurse team then it may well be that dying at home can be possible. Either don't go in to hospital in the first place (you have every right to refuse to do so!) or let it be known that you want to go home to die.

Most hospital staff, in conjunction with community GP's and District Nurses will move heaven and earth to get someone home to die if that is what the person wants and it is feasible. And therein lies the problem, it needs to be feasible. If you need constant care and you have no one to give it, then it is unlikely that you will be going home to die. Because we can't allow people to die on their own and/or uncared for can we? As we're getting towards the end and our physical faculties are bidding us goodbye, it is useful to have someone to empty commodes or provide a mouthful of warm soup or put another blanket on the bed. It's just not upholding our 'duty of care' as professionals to allow people home to be alone at this time. If help is available, to empty catheter bags and give a sip of tea, to wipe a fevered brow and hold a hand then yes, it can be arranged and quite swiftly too if there are the requisite number of staff available. If those at home with you are confident they can manage the care needs to help you (not everyone needs a lot of physical care though the huge majority need some), there is no reason you can't go home to die. Equipment such as hospital beds and mattresses can be organised fairly swiftly (this is called 'fast tracking', ie. trying to do everything swiftly to allow the patient to go home in what limited time may be available to them, exactly how fast it is depends on a number of factors including availability of staff and equipment) and if care staff are needed and if the agencies have the available staff then it can all happen in a number of hours. Realistically and much more likely is that it will take a few days to organise. Nonetheless it is a fantastic service if it is able to work smoothly and hospital staff are glad that they have been able to do their bit to give the patient what they want. So being very unwell and knowing you are going to die in hospital does not mean you can't go home but think about this…is it feasible? Make your wishes known as soon as appropriate, tell the nurses or the doctors or both to give everyone time to get things organised. They want to help you but they are not mind readers. Also bear in mind that not everyone wants to die at home, some folk like the security that being in a hospital can bring, so don't assume that staff will automatically think that you want to go home and be organising it behind the scenes. Be up front about your wishes and make them known to everyone who is involved in your care.

If one doesn't die at home, where else is a good option? Well, hospices are establishments set up to help those who are dying to achieve the best end possible and they have such a lot of experience in this stage of life. Moreover, most hospices are purpose built so every thought has gone into what would make a dying person and their family comfortable. Bigger, airier rooms, a garden view, possibly the ability to wheel the bed out into the garden, some are welcoming of dogs or pets that can travel, ability for family to stay in the same room with the dying person. The expertise and caring is second to none and they aim to treat everyone individually so taking account of personal preferences. One doesn't have to be dying of cancer to be accepted by a hospice, a terminal diagnosis of any disease state is sufficient though bear in mind that availability for treatment and care in these establishments is often in short supply. Any patient accepted by the hospice for treatment must be aware of their diagnosis. The vast majority of hospices and cancer specific services are funded by charities and so reliant on public support to keep them going.

In more rural or less populated areas, some hospices will also run a 'Hospice at Home' service and though these vary in the amount of care they can provide due to funding or staffing, they all aim to allow a person to stay at home to die and give specialist 'palliative' care [154]. Other agencies that can provide care at home in the last days are Marie Curie Care [155] (again charitably funded and also not cancer specific) or Macmillan Cancer Support [156]. As these are charitably funded, I can't detail here all the services they can provide as it will depend on how many people they are supporting at home, how many staff they have, what their resources are, but...they are there to help and they will do their utmost to do so.

The local hospital is also a possibility and is very often the place where people die. If it becomes apparent that a patient is dying then staff will attempt to move them into a side room if only to give them and their nearest and dearest a bit of peace and quiet and privacy for this stage (hospitals are amongst the noisiest places on earth I think). Side rooms in hospitals are at a premium as anyone with an infective condition that poses a threat to others will also need to be nursed in a side room. Thus, it is not impossible that a patient gets moved to another ward where a room is available. It is unfortunate that one hears people wondering if they're being moved because they're going to a ward to die; not the case, it is the lack of rooms available that prompts a move. That's all. The staff on the original ward would far rather keep the patient, they know and have built up a relationship with that person and their family and friends and regardless of what you think of nurses, they do have an emotional interest in their patients. So whilst it's probably not someone's location of preference, many of us will die in hospital, either a District General or with a bit of luck the local Community Hospital. Staff in hospitals have access to specialist knowledge that helps people have a peaceful end. The Trust that is in charge of that hospital will have a Palliative Nurse Specialist who is able to advise on symptom management and best practice. A lot of people die in hospitals and find comfort from the presence of the professionals around them. If you are dying in hospital and there is no-one to be with you, no family, no friends, folk can't get in to see you or it looks like it's going to happen a lot sooner than was anticipated...then if possible, someone will sit with you. Hold your hand if that's what you seem to want. Maybe read from the Bible or the religious source relevant to your religion to you if they know that would be appropriate. Mop your brow and make you comfortable, let you know that you are a member of the great human tribe and someone else is there to witness and comfort you on this next stage. I have known staff from Student Nurses to Health Care Support Workers, the Chief Nursing Officer of

---

[154] Rees-Roberts, M, Williams, P., Hashem, F., Brigden, C., Greene, K., Gage, H., Goodwin. M., Silsbury, G., Wee, B., Barclay, S., Wilson, P.M. and Butler, C., 'Hospice at Home services in England: a national survey', *BMJ Supportive & Palliative Care* 2019; **0**:1-7, doi:10.1136/bmjspcare-2019-001818 Accessed 2nd December 2023

[155] https://www.mariecurie.org.uk/ Accessed 2nd December 2023

[156] https://www.macmillan.org.uk Accessed 2nd December 2023

the hospital and the Senior Nurse on call for the day do this service...because it is part of our role and it is also our privilege.

And for some of us, we will die elsewhere, anywhere where normal life goes on. As not all of us know that our end is near and some deaths are sudden, there can be no planning in advance for the ultimate 'goodbye'. Having stuff prepared in advance may be useful (regardless of your age or state of health). Here I would suggest writing out letters to your children saying the stuff you would like to say on your deathbed just in case you're denied that final scene. Keeping your paperwork and documentation in reasonable order, beneficial both for you and for those left bereaved who will need to deal with the 'stuff' of your life left behind. Ensuring it's easy for everyone to find their way through your ephemera to get to the information they need (a file or big envelope with the relevant papers in can be useful here).

How

When thinking of dying most people are frightened of pain and being unable to breath well enough and how it will be to no longer be alive. To deal with the first, there are any number of pain killers that can be used to help a dying person be without pain, mostly they are an opioid based analgesia as by the time one is at this stage of a painful disease process, opioids are the only thing that cut it. If one is allergic or has a bad reaction to opioid medication, there are synthetic alternatives available that are equally as useful. These drugs may be mixed in a syringe with anti-sickness medication and also medicine that dries up secretions if they are proving a problem. Sometimes an anti-anxiety medication can also be added if that is proving difficult too. The contents of the syringe can be gently infused into the patient, just under the skin, via a device called a 'syringe driver', they are small battery powered devices and discreet enough to be hidden under sheets or pillows. If you are at home then the District Nurse may well take over management of it, or if you are paying for nursing care then the nurse you have employed or if you are having a Macmillan nurse, they too will know how to deal with it. In hospitals or hospices, the nursing staff will manage it. The contents are changed every twenty-four hours and if the amount of medication is not enough then the prescription can be altered to allow for an increase in the appropriate drug and/ or sometimes a 'top up' injection can be given. The aim in this is to keep the patient pain free, anxiety free and as comfortable as possible at all times through this process.

By the time the end is near, if pain is a problem, then the syringe driver route is probably the one that most professionals in concert with their patient will choose. If the dying person has difficulty swallowing or is beyond that stage in their life then it is one of the best routes of getting medication into someone and alleviating their pain. There are other methods but they are very old fashioned and fairly undignified (suppositories of some analgesics are available) so have decreased in use, nonetheless they are there if needed. Nurses are trained to recognise when folk are in discomfort even if the patient is no longer able to say so... and will alert the doctor that the prescription needs changing so don't allow fear of pain to concern you.

Shortness of breath is also a common around dying, especially and understandably for those with respiratory conditions. There are drugs also to deal with this. And happily, some of the pain killing drugs are also ones that help with breathing. Part of the natural process of dying is that the body lessens in its' desire to keep itself going. In the days or hours beforehand though, there can be a shortness of breath leading to this understandable worry and this can be dealt with by drugs (used in the syringe driver I mentioned above or as a patch on the skin or as a little tablet that dissolves whilst held in the mouth between gum and upper lip) but as the process continues, the breathing changes, things get a lot easier. The sensation of being short of breath can also be relieved by such routine things as opening a window to allow a breeze into the room or using an electric fan to waft air around, sitting the person up so that the lungs get a good amount of expansion also helps.

The existential worry is common to us all, I refer you to an article dealing with this subject which I have already used as a reference [157]. For some faith will provide a comfort in this time, for others of us…not so much. Thinking about it in advance is useful as having come to terms with the idea of it all will save angst at the time. For those of a particular faith, the staff of the hospital, hospice, residential home, wherever you are will call in a religious leader or faith fellow should you require spiritual sustenance. As far as is possible, your significant others will be encouraged to be with you if they can. Remember you're the star of the show here, let others know how you want it to be.

To help

I am going to mention a proforma that used to be known as the 'Liverpool Care Pathway', a set of suggested actions prescribed (originally in Liverpool but disseminated country wide) to alleviate symptoms and promote an easy and comfortable death. Unfortunately it got a bad press as some folks were concentrating a little too much on the pathway bit and a little too less on the care part of it [158]. Nonetheless, a version of this in altered form still exists although it is no longer called a 'pathway' (as that implies there is only one way to go whereas all nurses have seen folk return from death's door). It is nowadays known as Guidance for Care Decisions in the Last Days of Life, or something similar depending whereabouts you live and what health authority/ trust/nation looks after you. The one I am looking at as I write this, has on the very front page, that decisions of care should be discussed with the patient if possible and with the patient's significant others so that everyone knows what is happening and decisions are made in the clear light of day. It has a couple of pages of patient symptom assessments so that a note of any symptoms can be kept and importantly, dealt with. There is also a prescription chart provided so that a doctor can prescribe the relevant drugs and it even reminds the medic that certain medication should be considered. This document is about making decisions rationally, with the patient or the patient's family in accord and aware of the likely prognosis. Also included are sections on hydration and nutrition as often as the end of life approaches, the body appears to want less nourishment and hydration.

---

[157] Lewis R., *Facts to Calm Your Fear of Death and Dying*, Nov 22nd 2018, accessed via https://www.psychologytoday.com on 2nd December 2023

[158] https://compassionindying.org.uk/ Accessed 4th December 2023

Decisions around those matters will be taken in consultation with the patient (if possible) and the patient's next -of-kin, again so that everyone understands what is happening and why. The aim of this is always, always, always to make this a comfortable process for the patient.

Afterwards

Dying can be a long and slow process that will give you time to say all you need or want to say to those around you, have a glass or two of champagne if that's your thing (not unknown), gather all your important folk around and have a bit of a get together really. Conversely it may happen suddenly (for all that you have been ill for a while) and you may not have time to do all the above. It is wise therefore to have made your will (see Chapter 3) because death bed wishes do not count in a court of law. If you want to be really tidy and organised you may well have arranged your own funeral or at least thought about it and have an idea of what you'd like to commemorate your life and achievements. There is no harm in thinking about this, maybe years, maybe decades in advance. It is not going to make it happen any sooner. If you know what you'd like to happen then either arrange it (and pay for it) in advance or let your nearest and dearest know so that they can get it sorted if that's what they want to do. There is always the possibility if you don't organise it yourself that it will be left to your most disorganised child to arrange as the rest of the family are prostrate with grief. Your choice. If you want to be buried, where would you like that to happen and how much will a plot cost? Will your estate cover that or is it too expensive? What sort of funeral would you like? Über posh and ornate, horses and black feathers or just a quiet and simple crematorium affair? Or nothing in the way of commemoration and service at all? Whatever you plan or want, no matter how fancy or how plain, how quiet or how noisy, remember that it is your family and friends last opportunity to express to you and to each other how much you meant to them. So, whilst you may have a lot of fun organising plotting and planning, don't forget what it's for. Give them an occasion to express their love and respect for you.

Normal forms of a funeral consist of the person in their coffin either being brought into the room/church/chapel/crematorium or being there whilst the mourners come in. A religious service will usually be taken by a leader of the faith with possibly sayings, poems, eulogies added in by other folk. A non-religious event can take whatever form folk want but there is a reason why the religious ceremonies are constructed in that way…because it gives people the opportunity to remember, to say goodbye, to share memories or appreciation, to collectively gather to acknowledge the death and loss of one of the tribe. If you are designing your own, bear in mind those functions.

Usual things involved in funerals are funeral directors though strictly speaking they are not necessary. However, they have the experience, the expertise, thorough knowledge of the law around the area, are able to liaise with religious or lay institutions that deal with funerals, know how it is all arranged, possibly have a few religious folk they know of who can lead a funeral, can sort out stationery and crematoriums, cars and coffins, get the relevant forms signed and generally make it work very smoothly so that the mourners can get on with mourning. They cost money of course, all that expertise isn't cheap but a way to spread the cost is to pre-pay, either in an advance lump sum or by regular payments...it means that the cost is covered, it's no worry for your significant other and if you pay well enough in advance, you end up getting it cheaper.

If you are the wife/ husband/ son/ daughter/ friend/ neighbour/ next of kin of the person who has just died then there are a few things you need to do legally. First is to register the death, this needs to be done within a certain time (five days for England, Wales and Northern Ireland; eight days in Scotland [159]). Note that it is illegal not to register the death [160]. Although usual for a close relative to register the death it doesn't have to be so; there are a few rules around it though. If not a relative then someone who was present when the person died, or who lives in the house or an official in the building where the person died or the person arranging the funeral (but not the Funeral Director) [161]. A medical certificate of the cause of death will be issued by the GP or the hospital or hospice doctors depending on where the person died; this is not the official 'Death Certificate'. This certificate is necessary to register the death. Registration happens at the Registry Office, the same where you go to celebrate a marriage or register a birth and you'll usually need to make an appointment to do so [162]. It is actually free to register the death but if you want the official certificate you need to pay for it, prices vary from office to office. It takes about half an hour and you'll be given the posh 'Death Certificate' to keep with family documents and importantly to let the funeral director have sight of so that they can arrange to collect and prepare the body. You will also need copies of the Death Certificate (not photocopies, they want the real McCoy given by the Registry Office) to give to banks, insurance or pension companies, the land registry if there is title to property, any of the myriad of institutions who will want and need to know about the death. It is thus worth getting a few extra from the Registry Office at the time as although it is possible, it is a fag to have to get them later and may hold up part of the proceedings. There is a service run by gov.uk that will alert all the necessary government departments of the death of the person, accessed on Tell Us Once (though not available in Northern Ireland at present) [163]. When you register the death, the Registrar will either give you a specific reference number to input into the Tell Us Once service or will go through it with you and fill it in there and then [164].

If the death of the person was unexpected or sudden, there is a legal duty to report the death to the Coroner or in Scotland, the Procurator Fiscal [165]. They may decide that further investigation is

---

[159] https://www.gov.uk/after-a-death/ Accessed 4th December 2023

[160] https://www.citizensadvice.org.uk/family/death-and-wills/what-to-do-after-a-death/ Accessed 4th December 2023

[161] https://www.bereavementadvice.org/topics/registering-a-death-and-informing-others/who-can-register-a-death/ Accessed 4th December 2023

[162] https://www.bereavementadvice.org/topics/registering-a-death-and-informing-others/ Accessed 4th December2023

[163] https://www.gov.uk/after-a-death/organisations-you-need-to-contact-and-tell-us-once and https://www.nidirect.gov.uk/articles/who-tell-about-death Accessed 4th December 2023

[164] https://www.gov.uk/after-a-death/organisations-you-need-to-contact-and-tell-us-once Accessed 4th December 2023

[165] https://www.gov.scot/publications/death-scotland-practical-advice-times-bereavement-revised-11th-edition-2016-9781786522726/pages/5/ Accessed 4th December 2023

needed and the medical certificate of cause of death will not be issued until they are satisfied that they have met their legal duties in this matter. Thus, it may be that with a sudden or unexpected death of a person, there is no quick or timely funeral and the process of saying goodbye to that person becomes long and drawn out. Various religions have differing opinions on the speed at which a body should be buried and all public servants and bureaucratic offices will do their best to meet their requirements BUT their duty of care is to the deceased, to ensure their death was natural or explained. So, if you are in the position of dealing with the untimely death of a loved one / family member/ close friend and it becomes long and drawn out, you may be on intimate acquaintance with the grief for a long time. Conversely, leaving a funeral for a little while to allow mourners to gather from all parts of the globe is also possible. Most funerals take place within a few weeks of the persons death but there is no strict timetable on this one [166]. The Funeral Director will be able to advise.

Conclusion

This is a fairly short chapter and I've included some resources below to allow further investigation. I hope I have managed to convey some comfort or at least provoked a bit of planning around the subject. What I have not included is dealing with bereavement, and that's not because I don't think it's a valid subject but one I think is way beyond my scope and knowledge to expertly write.

Useful websites and resources

https://www.citizensadvice.org.uk/
A registered charity with a web site that will lead you specifically to the nation in which you require information before dealing with it. Helpful because things do differ between devolved nations. Their remit is pretty wide and covers money, debt, law, health, benefits, housing, dealing with death and registration and also any grants or benefits that may be paid. There is an advice link service, a free phone call on 0800 702 2020, available 09:00 hrs to 17:00 hrs. Postal address is Citizen's Advice, 3rd Floor North, 200, Aldersgate, LONDON, EC1A 4HD

https://compassionindying.org.uk
Set up to help people with an information line and very much focused on helping people fill out their Advance Decisions, their aim is to help plan for eventualities. Postal address is 181, Oxford Street, LONDON, W1D 2JT and their phone number is 0800 999 2434

---

[166] https://www.dignityfunerals.co.uk/advice/how-long-after-death-does-a-funeral-typically-take-place/ Accessed 4th December 2023

https://www.dignityfunerals.co.uk

A business of some 800 funeral directors who aim to set the highest standards for funeral care and who have various undertaking establishments in the UK. They have a 'find an undertaker' function and they do pre-paid funerals.

https://www.gov.uk/

...is a treasure trove of information though it isn't particularly attractively presented. Nonetheless, a good trawl through this website can turn up all sorts of interesting things. In this chapter I've concentrated on dealing with death and registration of such and the legalities around this matter.

https://www.hospiceuk.org

A charity that works "...for the benefit of people affected by death and dying..." and the site deals with all things hospice including a useful hospice finder, support for those dealing with bereavement, and educational material. Their address is Hospice UK, 34-44 Britannia Street, LONDON, WC1X 9JG

https://www.macmillan.org.uk   A charity that supports people with cancer, offering support financially, emotionally and with physical matters. Their support line is on 0808 808 00 00 and their postal address is Macmillan Cancer Support, 89, Albert Embankment, LONDON, SE1 7UQ.

https://www.mariecurie.org.uk Initially set up as a charity to help those with cancer it has widened it's remit to include all persons with terminal illnesses, runs hospices and funds research. They provide (resources permitting) nursing at home as well. Postal address is Marie Curie, 89, Albert Embankment, LONDON, SE1 7TP and the helpline is reached on 0800 920 2309

CONCLUSION

Well this has been a whistle stop tour of the travails of getting older hasn't it? I hope it's not been too alarmist for you but that instead you've taken information that has proved useful and had a think, maybe changed a few ways of doing things or perhaps put some form of plan into action. It has never been my intention to scare anybody but instead to enable folk to take control of a process that if we're lucky, won't happen to us, but statistically is likely. It isn't age we have to fear but ill health and deteriorating faculties. It is those that cause the problems and a reluctance to face up to and deal with them in a timely manner that leads to trouble. If nothing else I expect this book has brought that to your attention.

I have dealt with the practicalities of literally getting your house in order so as to make it easier to stay where you are (if you like living there) or to think about changing your abode now so that you can savour a new place to live. Do it early and enjoy the process of moving or changing, leave it till later and it becomes an energy sapping trial. Likewise little things, small changes that can help, changes of domestic order or getting the rugs taken up; get them done now to make life easier later and to prevent mishaps.

I talked also about the people there are available to help you and their roles, how you can access their expertise. Seek help earlier rather than leaving it till the last minute, too little and too late is of no use to anyone. These people are here to aid you but unless you contact them; they will not know that you need their help. With all of these professions, if they feel they are unable to assist but another specialist will be of better service to you, they will tell you.

The legal stuff and the chapter around wills, advance directives, packages of care, next of kin and Power of Attorney I wrote to give you pause for thought and at least swept away a few mistaken beliefs around the subject. Early action on these matters will pay off, as some of this legal stuff takes weeks and months to action. It is defiantly a case of getting it in place in case you need it but hoping you never will.

Coming into contact with hospitals is statistically more likely as we get older hence the chapter on hospitals and hospital visits. The nature of those places is changing. It is no longer a jolly caper from 'Carry on Doctor', they are busy, noisy places with an ideology of rescue that find themselves dealing with social cares more often than not. They are doing their best with too few staff and resources in an age and expectation of technical ability to keep life going at all costs. At least I alerted you to the need for ear plugs!

The failing senses and the adjuncts that can make life better have been all too briefly talked about in Chapter Two. Early action pays off rather than leaving it to the last minute when sensory impulses have been lost. Equipment and the various sorts of aids you may need or be given to help with mobility were also mentioned.

In Chapter Six I talked about various activities of living including sex and diet, keeping one's physical body at it's best through activity and medication, dealing with pain and the difference between an intolerance and an allergy. It's a chapter that could've been three or four times the size but I had to rein in somewhere and didn't want to overload anyone with information.

And in my last chapter I dealt with dying with the aim of lessening some of the fears that folk have around the matter, I talked a little about hospices and home care, about pain and anxiety relief and what a syringe driver is. It's not obligatory reading that last chapter and some people won't like the idea of it at all, but it may provide a bit of reassurance to some.

Whilst I have dealt with the ails of getting older in an effort to alert you, don't think that being an elder is all about ill health and misery. So many people of advanced years have fun and a fulfilled life, doing what they want to do in the manner they wish to do it. Many, many folk have adapted their lives in a way that lets them do the things they love in a safe manner and with less worry, so they can carry on living at home amongst the possessions they love in an area where they find community, health and happiness.

Really it's been a very surface skim of how to live well as an elder. There are lots more areas I could've dealt with. But too much of a good thing is still too much, hence the reason I kept this book pretty short. My aim of course is that lots of people read and find this useful. But, you know what? If only one person reads this and takes on board things I've suggested and finds their life is a little better subsequently, then it'll have been a process worth doing.

Printed in Great Britain
by Amazon